nadiya bakes

For Abdal

If you didn't eat cake, who would I bake cake for?

This cake was always going to be for you.

NADIYA BAKES

nadiya hussain

photography by **chris terry**

clarkson potter/publishers
new york

contents

introduction

As first loves go, I have many. We all have many.

For fifteen-year-old me, it was the Backstreet Boys, who I was going to meet one day (so I told myself) and I would marry Kevin, though not before all five of them battled to win my love! Even now, at thirty-five, they still send my heart aflutter because out of all the bands that fifteen-year-old girl could have loved, they were the first.

But back here in real life, away from the land of make-believe and distant teenage dreams, I have had the joy of many weird and wonderful first loves. Becoming a proper older sister, when my baby brother was born, my first taste of maternal, yet not technically maternal, love. That was a first love of many to come. My first real pet, Hira the cat, she loved me like tuna and I loved her like I love chips. Becoming an aunt for the very first time, that rush of connection—we share the same DNA and I didn't even have a hand in making him. That was a first love.

My first secondhand bike I shared with my sisters; her name was Bluebird and she was blue, rusty, with white tires and cost my dad 25 cents from a Sunday market. I loved that bike, but that unpadded seat did not love me! My first pair of roller skates, yes they were hand-me-downs and I grew out of them pretty quickly, but they rolled me to places beyond the parameters set by parental guidance, not far but far enough, so my blades I loved.

Finding love, actual real love, nothing like anyone else's and all our own. Real, first, true, actual love. And children: real people, growing inside me, waiting to be met. You would think that first love of seeing one's child would change, fade, or lessen with each subsequent child, but no. It's still there, first love, fresh love, new love, every single time, with every single child.

And then of course there is cake. Yes, cake.

You may ask, how can cake sit here in this list? This list of monumental events and material memories, where does cake fit here? Like everything on my list of first loves, baking came into my life at a particular point, but unlike my memories of boy bands, roller-blades, and pets, which sit somewhere in "things that once were," baking is right here with me still. With my husband, with my children, with my family. Baking has become such a massive part of who I am that there is no denying it. I live it, I breathe it, I whisk, stir, measure, and bake it! For goodness' sake, I dream about it! I really do.

Baking is my first love.

I didn't quite realize it when as a teenager I baked a cake for my sister's pre-wedding party. A simple cake, sandwiched together with sticky jam and groaning under the sheer weight of thick white fondant and a hideous fondant groom all dressed in his fondant finery. I didn't see it when I did a GCSE in Food Studies a few years later and designed an entire Pokémon Cake, with marbled red-and-white layers, sand-wiched with jam and covered in a colored fondant, shaped and cut carefully to create an actual "Poké Ball." The teacher said, "You're really good at baking. Ever considered going to catering college?" I'm also

good at tying my shoelaces, so who cares?! I thought. I just wanted an A in Food Studies, and that I got. But still nothing—the connection wasn't there. Whatever it is I have now, whatever I feel now, it didn't ignite, it didn't even spark.

We had an oven at home, but it was full of pans; it wasn't used for baking, just for storing greasy deep-frying pans, and I never really saw it any other way. It was a cupboard NOT an oven. Life happened around all of that—I got married and we got our own house and even our own oven. Still nothing, not an urge, not a spark, not a thought to bake. Until . . .

"Can you bake, because I love cake?" I supposed I *could* bake, maybe just a little, for him. I gave it a try. It started with a wonky cake, and he ate the whole thing. So I saved for an oven thermometer to make sure the oven temperature was regulated. The next cake was less wonky. Still delicious and he ate it again! Then some strawberry and cream muffins. A whole dozen. A little chewy, not very cake-like, tasty though, and he ate them all. By then the babies joined in too. I saved a few strawberries out of sight in the back of the fridge and tried again. Mixed the mixture a little less. There was a definite improvement. They were eaten even faster than the ones that came before.

And before I knew it I was baking bread, enriching doughs, making pastry, laminating, making starters—and killing starters! I was baking every day, all because I had someone to eat it. Baking became a part of life, like cooking, like laundry, like vacuuming, like breathing. It was just natural, it was normal. And it was loved.

So nothing gives me greater pleasure than to finally be able to share this beautiful book with you. I could have begun writing this book and never really stopped, but the powers that be said I had to! So I did. But not till I had put together some of my favorite recipes—traditional, twisted, and everything in between. This book is a compilation of all the yummy ideas that fly around in my head and all the things my husband eats over and over again.

Let me take you through the chapters. Cakes, Mini Cakes & One-Pan Bakes: if you're in this chapter, I would highly recommend the "money can't buy you happiness brownies." If you're in the No-Bake Bakes chapter, well you guessed right: no baking but still "baking" with the banana ice cream cheesecake with blueberry compote. Tarts & Pies: this is filled with all sorts of delights, from a sweet carrot tart to a rainbow veg pakora picnic pie. Desserts: you'll need a spoon in this chapter, if you're eating the roasted fruit cobbler or the croissant ice cream pudding. Every baker needs a good Celebration Bake and there are plenty to pick from. It could be a sit-in-the-middle-of-the-table cranberry and chile brioche wreath or a celebratory praline king cake. We can't have a baking book without a Breads chapter, full of Cornish splits and pulled chicken doughnuts. Cookies, we've got to have cookies, be they coffee meringue bark or rhubarb and custard butter kisses! If you fancy a Savory Bake there are baked chile churros and a cauliflower cheese lasagne. There is something in this book for all of us for every occasion—not that we need an occasion to turn on the oven!

Many people may read this and not get it. But for those of you who love baking as much as I do, you will get it instantly, and that's why you now have this book in your home. Baking doesn't have to be your first love, or indeed anywhere in a long list of loves like mine, but perhaps it's waiting to become one of yours, and maybe you'll find just the recipe in here to ignite the love or at the very least fuel it.

Bake, eat, love, repeat!

chapter one

CAKES,
MINI CAKES &
ONE-PAN BAKES

———

turmeric and ginger diamonds

Makes approx. 24 diamonds
Prep 20 minutes   Cook 30 minutes
Will keep for 5 days in a tin

For the cake

⅓ cup/100g tahini

3⅔ cups/450g all-purpose flour, sifted

1¾ cups/360g granulated sugar

2½ teaspoons ground ginger

2½ teaspoons ground turmeric

½ teaspoon baking powder

½ cup + 2 tablespoons/145ml good olive oil

1¾ cups/420ml boiling water

1 x 4-inch piece of crystallized ginger, very finely chopped

For the top

1 tablespoon sesame seeds

1 tablespoon pine nuts

¼ cup/60ml honey

This is my take on a traditional Lebanese treat. The turmeric smells savory, but in fact it brings a sweetness to the recipe, and I have also added ginger to really complement the turmeric, so your senses will be very busy. These look beautiful and are so simple to make, topped with pine nuts and sesame seeds for some crunch. Perfect if you want something a little bit different.

Start by preheating the oven to 350°F. Have a 9 x 13-inch/23 x 33cm baking pan ready, lined with parchment paper.

Put the tahini straight into the bottom of the baking pan and, using a pastry brush, brush the sides and edges until they are completely covered.

Combine the flour, sugar, ground ginger, turmeric, and baking powder in a bowl and whisk till mixed.

Make a well in the center and add the olive oil, then the boiling water, then the crystallized ginger and mix until you have a beautifully fragrant yellow batter, thick enough to pour.

Now pour the mixture into the tahini-lined pan—it should all run into a smooth, even layer. Sprinkle the sesame and pine nuts all over the top.

Bake for 30 minutes, until firm to the touch. Take it out of the oven and let cool for 10 minutes before using a small serrated knife to cut diagonal lines in opposite directions, still in the pan, to form diamonds.

Brush all over with the honey.

Allow to cool completely in the pan before serving.

blueberry and lavender scone pizza

Makes 12 wedges   **Prep** 25 minutes
Cook 15 minutes   **Best eaten** straightaway

For the scone

2¾ cups/350g all-purpose flour, sifted, + a little extra for dusting

¾ teaspoon salt

5 teaspoons baking powder

6 tablespoons/85g unsalted butter, softened

¼ cup/45g granulated sugar

1 teaspoon dried lavender, crushed

1 lemon, finely grated zest only

¾ cup/175ml whole milk, room temperature

For the topping

2 x 8-oz/227g jars of clotted cream or crème fraîche

1 teaspoon vanilla bean paste

5 tablespoons/100g blueberry jam

1 cup/180g fresh blueberries

finely grated zest of half a lemon

These scone wedges are made in one big circle, just like a pizza. I am forever getting involved in the what-goes-first debate (cream or jam?), though to be honest, as long as neither is left off, I'm a happy girl. I once vowed never again to bake with lavender after an epic flavor disaster, but I have since learned that a little goes a long way. So, don't be tempted to diverge from the quantities here, or you WILL regret it!

Preheat the oven to 400°F and line a large baking sheet with parchment paper.

Pop the flour into a large bowl, along with the salt and baking powder, and mix well. Add the butter and rub it into the flour using your fingertips until there are no large traces left. Add the sugar, dried lavender, and lemon zest and mix.

Make a well in the center and add the milk. Using a rubber spatula, mix until it starts to form a dough. Gently bring the dough together with your hands. Tip it out onto a lightly floured surface and form the dough into a mound, but resist the temptation to knead or the scone will become chewy rather than soft and crumbly.

Put the mound into the center of the prepared sheet—this just saves a messy transfer once the dough is rolled out. Using a rolling pin or the back of your hand, press the dough out to an 8-inch/20cm circle about ¾ inch/2cm thick. If you want, trim the edges, though I prefer not to as I like the edges rough.

Now, using a sharp knife, cut the circle like a pizza into 12 slices, cutting all the way down and all the way through. Pop into the oven and bake for 15 minutes. The scone should be golden around the edges, a little less so toward the center, and firm to the touch.

Let cool completely on the sheet. As soon as it is cool enough, pop it onto your chosen serving dish.

Mix the clotted cream and vanilla bean paste together. Add the jam and ripple it through.

Spread the mixture all over the scone, leaving a ½-inch/1cm gap around the edge. Top with blueberries, scatter with lemon zest, and you are ready to serve!

tahini cake with banana curd

For the cake

butter, for greasing

⅔ cup/200g tahini

1 cup/200g granulated sugar

4 large eggs

1 medium banana, squashed to a paste

1⅔ cups/200g all-purpose flour, sifted

3½ teaspoons baking powder

¼ teaspoon salt

1 teaspoon vanilla extract

For the curd

4 large eggs

¼ cup/60g unsalted butter, softened

2 tablespoons lemon juice

1½ cups/300g granulated sugar

4 medium bananas, ripe, about 14 oz/400g

1 tablespoon cornstarch

½ teaspoon ground nutmeg

For the crunch

2 x 1-oz/30g packages of sesame crunch, crushed

Serves 8–10 **Prep** 40 minutes **Cook** 1 hour

This cake is made with tahini, so it is deliciously light and—like most of us—subtly nutty! The banana curd is scented lightly with nutmeg, so it's sweet with a bit of depth—again like most of us. Sesame brittle adds a crunch in places. I think we have established that we are all a little bit tahini cake with banana curd!

Start by lining an 8½ x 4½-inch/900g loaf pan with some parchment paper and lightly greasing it. Preheat the oven to 325°F.

Put the tahini, sugar, eggs, banana, flour, baking powder, salt, and vanilla into a large mixing bowl and whiz together with electric beaters for 2 minutes, until the mixture is smooth and glossy. Pour into the prepared loaf pan and level off the top.

Bake in the oven on the middle shelf for about 1 hour, until it has domed, is a light brown, and a skewer inserted comes out clean.

While it bakes, make the curd by putting the eggs, butter, lemon juice, sugar, bananas, cornstarch, and nutmeg into a food processor and blitzing to a smooth paste. You may need to do this step in two batches, depending on the size of your food processor.

Transfer the mix into a nonstick pot and place over medium heat, stirring all the time, until the mixture has thickened. Take it off the heat, transfer to a bowl, and let cool completely, then cover with plastic wrap and chill in the fridge.

As soon as the cake is ready, take it out and allow it to cool on a wire rack.

Cut the cooled cake twice horizontally, so you have three even layers. Set the top two layers aside and cover the bottom layer with two heaped tablespoons of curd, spread evenly. Sprinkle with a third of the crushed sesame crunch. Add the next cake layer and spread it with curd. Add another third of the crushed sesame crunch. Put the top layer of the cake back on and spread it with curd (about 5 tablespoons), then sprinkle with the rest of the crushed sesame crunch.

Any leftover curd will sit pretty in a jar in the fridge for 2 weeks. Perfect for pancakes!

matcha and kiwi hurricane roll

butter, for greasing

For the plain cake

5 large eggs (half will be for the matcha cake)

5 tablespoons/65g granulated sugar

½ cup/65g all-purpose flour, sifted

¾ teaspoon baking powder

pinch of salt

For the matcha cake

5 tablespoons/65g granulated sugar

½ cup/60g all-purpose flour, sifted

4 teaspoons matcha powder

For the filling

2 large kiwi fruit, peeled and roughly chopped

¼ cup/35g confectioners' sugar

½ cup/120ml heavy cream

Serves 6–8 **Prep** 40 minutes
Cook 15–18 minutes **Best eaten** on day it's made

This is a Swiss roll taken to the next level by adding a bright green ripple of matcha-flavored cake for an amazing hurricane effect. It's a thing of beauty! The distinctive matcha flavor in the cake is paired with a fruity kiwi cream in the center, and topped with a kiwi coulis. Too beautiful to eat? I think not.

Start by preheating the oven to 350°F, and grease and line a 9 x 13-inch/23 x 33cm baking pan with some parchment paper.

Now, begin making the plain cake. Crack the eggs into a liquid measuring cup and beat them with a fork to combine yolks and whites. There should be 1 cup/240ml total. Half will be for the plain cake and half for the matcha cake. Pour ½ cup/120ml of the beaten eggs into a large mixing bowl and whisk in the sugar until the mixture is really light and fluffy and the whisk leaves a trail when lifted—this is how you can tell it is thick enough. It should take 5 minutes using electric beaters.

Next, add the flour, baking powder, and salt and, using a rubber spatula, gently fold the mixture together until there are no trails of flour left and you have a smooth, airy batter.

Pour the mixture into the prepared pan and tilt it around to get the mixture into all the corners. Set it aside while you make the matcha mix.

Follow the same initial process as before, whisking the reserved ½ cup/120ml of beaten eggs and the sugar together until the mixture is thick and the whisk leaves a trail. Add the flour and matcha and fold gently together until you have a smooth, deep-green cake batter.

Pop the mixture into a piping bag—this will just make it easier to layer the green batter on top of the plain one in the pan without too much accidental mixing. Snip off the end and pipe the mixture over the top (see next page for the pattern).

→

Position the pan with the longest edge closest to you. Now take a butter knife, skewer, or a small rounded spoon and, starting at one corner, stick it in until it touches the bottom of the pan and run it through the batter all the way from end to end with one firm, continuous movement. When you get to the end, make a U-turn and go back, then another U-turn and back again, as if you are doing lengths of a pool, while gradually moving in a zigzag across the breadth of the whole pan.

Keep doing this until you have gone all the way across the pan.

Rotate the pan by 90 degrees so that now the shortest edge is closest to you and do the same in the other direction until you have gone all the way across.

Finally, give the pan two sharp taps on the worktop to help the mixture settle and make the top look more uniform.

Pop into the oven and bake for 17 to 20 minutes, until the center is springy to the touch.

Have ready a large sheet of parchment paper spread with a generous amount of granulated sugar.

As soon as you have taken the cake out of the oven, tip it out onto the sugared paper.

The cake will be sandwiched between two sheets of parchment paper; loosen the top sheet and then pop it back in place. Now, starting from the longer edge, roll up the whole thing, paper and all, and let it cool completely.

Next, make the filling by placing the kiwi in a food processor along with the confectioners' sugar and blitzing to a smooth paste.

Once the cake has cooled, unravel it, remove the top-most sheet of parchment paper, and spread half of the kiwi purée all over. Whisk the cream lightly, so it just holds its shape, then spread that over the kiwi in a thin layer. Now roll the whole thing back up again.

Reserve the rest of the kiwi purée for the top.

Take off the scrappy ends—they are for you, you're welcome! This just neatens up the roll so you can see the hurricane effect.

Pop onto a serving dish, drizzle over the rest of the kiwi purée in a line across the top, and let it drip. Slice the cake and you are ready to eat.

→

money can't buy you happiness brownies

Makes 18 squares
Prep 40 minutes, plus overnight chilling
Cook 1¼ hours   **Best kept** in the fridge for 3–4 days

For the brownie base

1⅓ cups/300g unsalted butter, + extra for greasing

10½ oz/300g dark chocolate

5 large eggs

1½ cups + 1 tablespoon/335g dark brown sugar

1 teaspoon instant coffee mixed with 2 teaspoons hot water

1 cup + 3 tablespoons/ 145g all-purpose flour, sifted

½ cup/35g cocoa powder, sifted

½ teaspoon salt

1 teaspoon all-purpose flour

1 cup/180g dark choc chips

For the nutty center

1⅓ cups/240g chopped mixed nuts or hazelnuts

2 x 9-oz/250g jars of dulce de leche

½ teaspoon salt

For the top

12¾ oz/360g full-fat cream cheese

½ cup + 2 tablespoons/ 120g granulated sugar

2 large eggs

1¼ teaspoons almond extract

finely grated zest of 1 orange

1 tablespoon all-purpose flour

cocoa powder, for dusting

I don't think I need to elaborate too much on these, do I? I am always in search of the best brownie, and I figure if you can't find it, make it. So here it is: a triple chocolate brownie, with a layer of toasted chopped nuts encased in dulce de leche, then topped with a zesty cheesecake mixture and baked again. I rest my case.

Put the butter and chocolate in a small pot and melt gently, stirring occasionally until the mixture is liquid. Set aside to cool.

Line the bottom and sides of a 9 x 13-inch/23 x 33cm baking pan with some parchment paper so that it comes ½ inch/1cm above the top of the pan, and lightly grease.

Preheat the oven to 350°F.

Combine the eggs, brown sugar, and cooled coffee in a large mixing bowl and whisk until the mixture is light, thick, and fluffy. This should take 5 minutes with electric beaters. (Adding the coffee really enhances the flavor of the cocoa and you won't even be able to taste the coffee itself.)

Pour in the cooled melted chocolate and whisk until the mixture no longer has any streaks in it.

Then add the sifted flour, cocoa, and salt and mix until you have a glossy batter.

Mix the teaspoon of flour with the chocolate chips in a bowl before mixing them into the batter until they're well dispersed—this trick will prevent them from sinking to the bottom when you bake the brownies. Pour the mixture into the prepared pan and level off the top. Bake for 25 minutes.

While it is baking, toast the nuts in a large nonstick pan, stirring until they are a deep golden brown.

Put the dulce de leche in a bowl along with the toasted nuts and the salt, mix, and set aside.

As soon as the brownies are baked, take them out of the oven and let cool completely in the pan. Spread the sticky nut mixture over the top and pop the whole thing in the freezer for 30 minutes.

Adjust the oven to 325°F.

Make the cheesecake top by mixing the cream cheese, granulated sugar, eggs, almond extract, orange zest, and flour together really well.

Spoon and spread into an even layer over the nut mixture and pop into the oven for about 50 minutes.

As soon as the cheesecake is set in the center, allow to cool totally and chill in the fridge overnight. The wait will be worth it!

Dust with the cocoa, take out of the pan, and cut into squares. Eat, eat, eat!

torta caprese
with caramelized white chocolate sauce

5 large eggs, separated

a pinch of salt

¾ cup + 2 tablespoons/ 200g unsalted butter, softened, + extra for greasing

¾ cup + 2 tablespoons/ 180g granulated sugar

2 cups/200g almond meal

7 oz/200g dark chocolate, melted

⅓ cup/25g cocoa powder

1 teaspoon baking powder

For the caramelized white chocolate

14 oz/400g good-quality white chocolate, broken into pieces

a pinch of salt

¾ cup + 2 tablespoons/ 150ml hot water

confectioners' sugar, for dusting

frozen summer fruit (optional)

Serves 8   **Prep** 30 minutes   **Cook** 1 hour, plus 45 minutes cooling   **Best eaten** while still a little warm but keeps well for 3 days

---

This is such a lovely chocolate cake, rich but light from whipped egg whites and yet with plenty of texture from the ground almonds. It's simple and delicious and so yummy served with warm caramelized white chocolate, as the only way my husband eats chocolate cake is with more chocolate on top!

Preheat the oven to 325°F and line and lightly grease a round 9-inch/23cm cake pan.

Begin with two medium bowls—separate the egg yolks and egg whites.

Add a pinch of salt to the egg whites and set aside.

Now take the bowl with the egg yolks and add the butter, granulated sugar, almond meal, cooled melted dark chocolate, cocoa powder, and baking powder.

Return to the egg whites. Using electric beaters, whisk until you have stiff peaks.

Now pop the beaters into the other mixture and whisk until you have a smooth, evenly blended chocolatey mixture.

Add a third of the egg white mixture into the chocolatey mix and mix in well with a spoon to loosen it.

Now add the rest of the egg white and gently fold in until you don't see any streaks remaining.

Pour into the prepared cake pan, level off the top, and bake for about 1 hour.

Now's a good time to begin making the caramelized white chocolate sauce to go with the torta.

Put the white chocolate and a pinch of salt into a large nonstick pan, big enough so the chocolate is in an even-ish layer. Pop the pan on low heat and allow the chocolate to melt completely.

Stir, and if all the chocolate has melted, spread out to an even, melted layer and turn up the heat just a fraction. Stir again and keep doing the same until all the chocolate is caramelized and an even golden color.

If the chocolate stiffens to a solid, chalky lump, remove from the heat and let cool undisturbed for a couple of minutes until it starts to melt again. Then return to the heat and continue spreading out and stirring. This whole process can take 20 to 25 minutes, and just as a warning, chocolate can get really hot, so be very careful. It is quite a lumpy mixture, so pop it into a pitcher or bowl, add the hot water, and whiz it with an immersion blender and that should give you a smooth, caramelized white chocolate sauce. The sauce will be very liquidy after you add the water, but it thickens as it cools.

Once the torta is baked it should be just firm in the center. Turn the oven off, open the door, and leave the torta in there for 30 minutes. Take out and let cool in the pan for another 15 minutes, then dust generously with confectioners' sugar. By generously, I mean totally covered! Slice and serve with the warm caramelized white chocolate and frozen summer fruit if you like.

If the sauce has cooled and become solid, you just need to reheat very gently in a pan or in a heatproof bowl over a pot of simmering water.

strawberry and clotted cream shortcake cupcakes

Makes 12 **Prep** 30 minutes, plus chilling **Cook** 15 minutes **Best kept** in the fridge for up to 2 days	

For the frosting

¾ cup/175g salted butter, softened

2¾ cups/350g confectioners' sugar

3½ oz/100g strawberry ice cream, softened

For the cake

12 round vanilla sandwich cookies

12 small strawberries, stems and leaves cut off

½ cup/110g clotted cream or crème fraîche

½ cup/110g granulated sugar

2 large eggs

1 teaspoon vanilla bean paste

¾ cup + 2 tablespoons/ 110g all-purpose flour, sifted

1¼ teaspoons baking powder

¼ teaspoon salt

⅓ oz/9g tube of freeze-dried strawberries to decorate

These are an American–British hybrid. I just can't settle on one flavor combo once I've thought of a way to combine several. Strawberries and cream is a classic, but I love clotted cream, so I couldn't resist using it to make the cake batter here: no butter, just cream! I also love strawberry short-cake, so under each cake is a cookie base, then a hidden strawberry inside, and I've topped it all off with strawberry ice-cream frosting! Why have just one thing when you can have it all?

Begin by making the frosting: Whisk the butter with electric beaters until pale and creamy. Sift in the confectioners' sugar. Stir with a spoon to roughly combine and then mix with the beaters until light and fluffy. Add the ice cream and beat until just combined. Chill in the fridge for at least 1 hour.

Whisk the chilled frosting until fluffy, then transfer to a piping bag fitted with a ½-inch/1cm star nozzle and put it back in the fridge.

Preheat the oven to 350°F and line a 12-hole muffin pan with some cupcake liners of your choice. To the bottom of each one, add a cookie, then top that with a whole strawberry, pointy bit facing up.

Now make the cake batter by combining the clotted cream and granulated sugar in a mixing bowl and beating them together until light and fluffy.

Add the eggs one at a time, mixing well after each one.

Add the vanilla bean paste, flour, baking powder, and salt and mix until you have a smooth batter.

Divide the mixture up among the 12 cupcake liners, making sure that each delicious strawberry is fully encased, until you have no batter left.

Tap the pan on the work surface to level off the batter and bake for 15 to 20 minutes, until the cupcakes are fluffy and golden.

Take out and let cool in the pan for 10 minutes before transferring them to a cooling rack.

Pipe the frosting onto the tops of the cupcakes and then sprinkle with the freeze-dried strawberries.

upside-down key lime cupcakes

Makes 12   Prep 30 minute, plus cooling
and chilling   Cook 25 minutes
Will keep in the fridge for up to 3 days

1 large lime, cut into 12 thin slices, then cut each slice in half

12 oat cookies or ginger-snaps (something that will fit the top part of the cupcake liner snugly)

whipped cream (optional)

For the cake

¼ cup/55g unsalted butter, very soft

¼ cup/55g granulated sugar

1 large egg

½ teaspoon vanilla extract

7 tablespoons/55g all-purpose flour, sifted

½ teaspoon baking powder

pinch of salt

For the lime custard layer

⅔ cup/200g condensed milk

1 large egg

2 limes, finely grated zest and juice

½ cup + 2 tablespoons/150ml heavy cream

These are inspired by key lime pie, but in cake form and a little bit upside down. Each one is layered up in a cupcake liner: lime, cake, zesty custard, and cookie, then baked and flipped over. All the same flavors as the famous pie, but literally turned on its head.

Start by preheating the oven to 350°F. Have a 12-hole muffin pan at the ready, lined with some cupcake liners. Place 2 lime half slices flat in the bottom of each cupcake liner.

Now make the cake batter by combining the butter, sugar, egg, vanilla, flour, baking power, and salt and beating until you have a light and shiny batter.

Using a small spoon, spoon a little batter into each cupcake liner until you have run out of mixture, making sure to keep them fairly equal. The batter is very thick, so you will need to use the back of the spoon to spread it to the edges of the liners.

Give the pan a few hard slams on the work surface to level the batter, then pop into the oven for 10 minutes.

When they are done, take them out and let cool in the pan. Lower the oven temperature to 325°F.

Make the lime filling by combining the condensed milk in a mixing bowl with the egg, the zest and juice of the limes, and the cream. Mix until the whole thing is slightly thickened, which will take about 30 seconds with electric beaters.

Now put about 1 tablespoon of this filling onto the top of each baked cake, doing your best to keep it fairly even.

Pop a cookie straight on top of each cake, pressing gently so the lime custard and cookie meet.

Bake in the oven for 15 minutes. Take out and let cool in the pan and then chill in the fridge for at least 1 hour before eating.

Peel off the cupcake liner and then turn each cupcake out onto its cookie base. I like to serve with a squirt of whipped cream—it's optional but delicious!

cornmeal cake with rhubarb and rosemary

For the cake

1 cup/220g unsalted butter, softened, + extra for greasing

1 cup + 2 tablespoons/220g granulated sugar

3 cups/300g almond meal

3 large eggs

1 orange, zested and juice reserved in a bowl for later

1 lemon, zested and juice reserved in same bowl as orange juice for later

1 rosemary sprig, leaves removed from the stalk and finely chopped

1 cup + 1 tablespoon/150g yellow cornmeal

1 teaspoon baking powder

1 large stalk of rhubarb (about 5 oz/140g), chopped into 1-inch/2.5cm pieces

For the syrup

½ cup/100g granulated sugar

6 tablespoons/50g confectioners' sugar

To serve

plain Greek yogurt

Serves 8–10 **Prep** 25 minutes
Cook 1 hour 20 minutes

When I was a child, my mum would cook rhubarb in curry and I loved it that way, so for a long time I thought of it as savory. When the school dinner lady plonked some on my plate one day for dessert, I didn't recognize it. But when you are single digits and a tomboy who's desperate to be girly, anything pink is worth a try. It was sloppy and stringy and tart and mainly just weird. After that, I disliked it for years. Hardly selling it, am I? But when it's treated right, rhubarb is delicious, and these days I adore it. Savory and sweet, it is one of my favorite things about the tail end of summer and the first days of autumn. Picked early, the flesh is perfectly pink! It's beautiful studded in this sweet and fragrant cake, which has a crunchy sugary crust on top.

Start by lightly greasing and lining an 8-inch/20cm round, removable-bottom cake pan with some parchment paper.

Preheat the oven to 350°F.

Combine the butter and sugar in a bowl and beat with electric beaters until the mixture is really light and fluffy. Now add the almond meal and mix well until there are no dry spots.

Add the eggs one at a time, making sure to beat well after each addition.

Now add the orange and lemon zest and the rosemary and mix thoroughly.

In a separate bowl, mix the cornmeal and the baking powder until they are well combined, then add them to the wet mixture and bring the whole thing together. As soon as you have a glossy yet grainy-looking texture you know it's ready.

Pour the mixture into the prepared pan and smooth to a level surface. Now dot your pieces of rhubarb evenly throughout. Make sure they are standing upright and push them straight in. As the cake bakes it will envelop these little sticks. Pop into the oven and bake for about 1 hour 20 minutes, until the middle is springy when tapped with a finger and a wooden skewer comes out with just a few crumbs attached. If the top of the cake is browning too much, cover it with a piece of foil.

While it bakes, in a small saucepan mix the granulated sugar with the juice from the orange and lemon and place onto high heat. As soon as the mixture comes to a boil, reduce the heat and allow it to become a thick syrup of about half the volume of liquid you started with. This should take about 10 minutes.

As soon as the cake comes out of the oven, pour the citrus syrup all over it and let cool for 5 minutes. Then dust the confectioners' sugar all over the top and allow it to soak into the syrup to form a delicious sugary top.

After about 20 minutes, take the cake out of the pan and pop onto a serving dish.

I love to serve this with simple Greek yogurt to balance out all those fragrant sweet flavors.

molasses anise madeleines with grapefruit syllabub

Makes 14–18 (and syllabub serves 5)
Prep 30 minutes Cook 20 minutes (when baked in two batches) Best eaten as soon as the chocolate sets or will keep in a tin for 2 days

For the madeleines

2 large eggs

½ cup/100g light brown sugar

1 tablespoon molasses, + a little extra for decoration

¼ teaspoon ground star anise—you can buy this pre-ground or grind a load up yourself

¾ cup/100g all-purpose flour, sifted, + extra for dusting

1 teaspoon baking powder

7 tablespoons/100g unsalted butter, melted and cooled, + extra for greasing the pan

5½ oz/150g dark chocolate, melted and cooled

For the syllabub

1¼ cups/300ml heavy cream

¼ cup/50g granulated sugar

finely grated zest and juice of ½ a grapefruit

Madeleines used to be my favorite as a kid, when our local Asian supermarket sold them for about a dollar a bag. Inside each bag, tumbled among one another, were these wonderfully scalloped, slightly dimpled golden cakes. I had to stop myself from eating the whole bag in one sitting, but when you're one of six kids, you do have to move fast! Madeleines are so simple to make and my version is sweet and molassesy, darker in color than the classic ones, with a tiny edge dipped in chocolate, and I also make a zesty grapefruit syllabub to dip them into.

Start by making the madeleine mixture. Combine the eggs, brown sugar, and molasses in a bowl and whisk until the mixture is light and fluffy. This should take 5 minutes using electric beaters.

Now add the star anise, flour, baking powder, and melted butter and mix well till you have a smooth cake batter. Set this aside and let rest for 20 minutes, uncovered.

Meanwhile you can be getting on with the syllabub. Combine the cream and granulated sugar in a bowl and whisk until the cream begins to thicken.

Now add the zest and juice of ½ a grapefruit and whisk until the cream comes to stiff peaks. Transfer to a serving dish, cover, and now the syllabub can go in the fridge until you're ready to eat.

→

Now preheat the oven to 400°F.

Grease the inside of a 12-hole madeleine pan, lightly flour, and tip out any excess. You want to make sure all the little grooves are covered—this will just ensure the cakes pop right out of the mold.

If you don't have a madeleine pan, you can use the inside of a shallow cupcake pan, greasing and flouring the same way, or you could use mini tartlet pans, again greasing and flouring as before.

Drop just enough mixture into the hole so it is about ¼ inch/½cm shy of the top.

Repeat this with all 12 and bake in the oven for 8 to 10 minutes, until each madeleine has a little dimple that's risen on top and they are a medium golden brown.

As soon as they are out of the oven, let them cool in the pan for 10 minutes. With the leftover batter, keep making more until you have no mixture left.

Allow them to cool, which shouldn't take long.

Have ready a sheet of parchment paper large enough to place all the madeleines on.

When they have cooled, dip a corner at an angle encasing just a third of the madeleine into the melted chocolate, and pop onto the parchment paper for the chocolate to set. Repeat with the rest.

Serve the madeleines alongside the chilled syllabub, giving it a drizzle of some extra molasses before eating!

covered-all-over lamington cake

Serves 10–12   Prep 45 minutes, plus cooling and setting   Cook 1 hour 10 minutes
Keeps for 2 days

For the cake

2¼ cups/285g all-purpose flour, sifted

1½ cups/300g granulated sugar

1 tablespoon baking powder

1 teaspoon salt

½ cup/120ml vegetable oil

7 large egg yolks

¾ cup/180ml water

2 teaspoons lemon extract

7 large egg whites

½ teaspoon cream of tartar

1 x 10½-oz/300g jar of seedless raspberry jam

2⅔ cups/250g dried shredded coconut

For the filling

¾ cup + 2 tablespoons/200g unsalted butter, softened

3¼ cups/400g confectioners' sugar, sifted

2 tablespoons whole milk

1 teaspoon vanilla extract

7 oz/200g marshmallows

I've never actually eaten a true Australian laming-ton, but I have had those fraudulent ones you get packed in a plastic tray. I was shocked to find they only had jam and coconut on the top, when I know for a fact that a proper lamington should be covered all over! So I've taken things into my own hands and created a cake version: light chiffon, smothered in jam, coated in dried shredded coconut, and filled to the brim with marshmallow buttercream. There you have it—a lamington, not in teeny-weeny squares, but ready to cut into wedges just the way I like, and covered, properly covered!

Begin by washing then thoroughly drying a 10-inch/25cm round cake pan, about 3 inches/7.5cm deep. It's important to remove all traces of grease so the cake can climb up the pan, rather than slide off. It feels counterintuitive when baking, but it's a must.

Preheat the oven to 325°F.

Combine the flour, sugar, baking powder, and salt in a bowl and mix well.

Make a well in the center and add the oil, egg yolks, water, and lemon extract. Set aside.

Put the egg whites and cream of tartar in another bowl and, using electric beaters, whisk till the mixture comes to stiff peaks.

Now, with the same beaters, whisk the flour and egg yolk mixture till you have a smooth batter.

→

Add one third of the egg white mixture to the batter and mix to loosen, using a metal spoon so you don't destroy all those air bubbles.

Now add the rest of the egg white mixture and fold in till you have a light, even, non-streaky cake batter.

Pour into the pan and bake for 55 minutes to 1 hour, until golden and firm on top.

Meanwhile you can be making your buttercream by combining the butter and confectioners' sugar in a bowl along with the milk and vanilla and whisking till smooth.

Now pop your marshmallows into a microwave-safe bowl and microwave for 30 seconds, till the marshmallows are puffy and doubled in size. This can take longer depending on the power of your microwave, so keep zapping in 5-second intervals till they are puffy, then take them straight out.

Add to the buttercream mixture straightaway and whisk till well combined. Pop into a piping bag and set aside.

Once the cake is done, take it out of the oven and turn it upside down onto a cooling rack. Let rest till the cake has cooled a bit. Once the pan is cool enough to hold, pop it off and allow the cake to cool completely.

Meanwhile, warm the jam till it is liquid—you can do this in a pan or in the microwave.

Spread the coconut in an even layer on a large baking sheet and bake in the oven for 12 to 15 minutes at 350°F, keeping an eye on it all the time and stirring occasionally, till the coconut is a light golden color. Take out and let cool on the sheet.

Spread the sides of the cooled cake generously with the jam. With one hand on the top and one on the bottom, lift the jammy cake and roll it in the sheet of coconut—this cake is sturdier than you'd think, so get it into that coconut, turning the whole time till all the sides are covered generously. Press the coconut into the jam, so it really glues itself on.

Now spread a layer of jam onto the top and sprinkle with a generous coating of coconut. Pop a baking sheet on top, put your hand under the cake, and flip it over.

You will need to get out the dustpan and brush is all I'm saying; there is no neat way of doing this!

There should be just the top side left to cover, so repeat the process with the jam and coconut, then pop the whole thing onto your chosen serving plate.

Let rest for 30 minutes to allow the jam to dry and the coconut to stick firmly.

Use a long, serrated knife to cut horizontally through the cake so you have two rounds, then pop the top one onto a baking sheet.

Pipe the delicious marshmallow buttercream into the exposed cake center, pop the other round on top, and you are good to go.

drenched rose cake

For the cake

¾ cup + 2 tablespoons/
200g unsalted butter,
softened, + extra
for greasing

1 cup/200g granulated
sugar

4 large eggs, lightly
beaten

1⅔ cups/200g
all-purpose flour, sifted

⅓ cup/40g pistachios,
crushed to a fine
powder

For the syrup

½ cup + 1 tablespoon/
200g golden syrup or
light corn syrup

7 tablespoons/100ml
water

3 cardamom pods,
seeds crushed

2 tablespoons rose syrup
or ½ to 1 teaspoon rose
water

1 heaped tablespoon
dried rose petals

vanilla ice cream
(optional)

Serves 8   **Prep** 30 minutes, plus cooling
Cook 35 minutes   **Keeps** in an airtight
container for 3–4 days

This is my take on a traditional Indian dessert called gulab jamun, in which balls of dough are fried to the point of almost being burned and then soaked in syrup. I've recreated the idea in cake form. My cake is deliberately overbaked (though not burned!) to produce a deep-golden exterior with a delicious flavor, in contrast to the simple butter cake inside. There's a hidden layer of pistachio and—as the name suggests—the cake is literally drenched in a sweet, sticky, cardamom and rose-infused syrup.

Start by preheating the oven to 400°F and generously greasing a 10-inch/25cm pie dish.

To make the cake batter, combine the butter and sugar in a large mixing bowl and beat until the mixture is really light and fluffy and very pale in color—it should almost be white. Now add the eggs a little at a time till everything is well combined. Tip in the flour (we're using no rising agents, because we want a dense cake) and mix until you have a smooth batter.

Pour half the mixture into the prepared dish and level off the top. Sprinkle the crushed pistachios over the surface of the batter, leaving a 1-inch/2.5cm gap around the edge. Gently press the nuts in with the back of a spoon. Then spoon the rest of the batter gently over the top and use a spatula or the back of a spoon to smooth it, making sure all the nuts are covered.

Pop into the oven for 35 minutes. This is the only time you don't have to worry about burning your cake! We want it to catch a little, especially around the edges.

Make the syrup by combining the golden syrup, water, crushed cardamom seeds, and rose syrup in a pan over high heat and bringing the mixture to a boil. As soon as it does, take it off the heat and add the rose petals to rehydrate.

As soon as the cake is done, take it out of the oven and cut it into eight wedges while it is still hot. Pour the syrup all over, concentrating especially on where you made those cuts. Let cool for about 30 minutes.

I love to eat this while it's still warm, with a big scoop of vanilla ice cream. Take a wedge and give it a go!

fudgy flapjacky fudge

Makes 36 pieces **Prep** 30 minutes, plus cooling
Cook 15 minutes **Store** in an airtight jar

1⅔ cups/150g rolled oats

1 teaspoon ground cinnamon

⅓ cup/50g currants

½ cup/115g unsalted butter, softened, + extra for greasing

2 cups + 2 tablespoons/ 450g brown sugar

½ cup + 2 tablespoons/ 150ml whole milk

1 x 14-oz/397g can of condensed milk

a pinch of salt

As you can see by the title of this recipe, I couldn't decide exactly what this is, so I will let you choose. I love flapjacks, the traditional oat bars popular in the UK, and I have a ritual that every time I put gas in the car (which isn't often, because I seem to like the thrill of running on empty while calculating whether I can make it to the next gas station—and it's always touch and go!), I always buy one of those flapjacks with a layer of yogurt on top. But even with the topping, they are just never sweet enough for me. I also love fudge but that can be toe-curlingly sweet. So, in my search for a middle ground, I decided to combine the two. Call it what you will, it's pretty yummy!

Start by putting the oats in a pan over medium heat and lightly toasting them. Keep stirring as you go and they will eventually become a golden brown—this can take 5 to 10 minutes.

Remove from the heat, add the ground cinnamon and currants, and mix, then set aside till later.

Lightly grease and line the base and sides of an 8-inch/ 20cm square baking pan with parchment paper. Next, combine the butter, sugar, milk, condensed milk, and a pinch of salt in a large nonstick pot. Place on medium heat and stir constantly until the sugar has dissolved.

Now bring to a boil, making sure to stir to prevent it from burning or sticking on the bottom.

Turn the heat down and simmer, stirring all the time, for 10 to 15 minutes. The mixture will begin to thicken and the bubbling on the surface will look a little slower. There are a few ways of working out when the mixture is hot enough to set: have an ice-cold bowl of water beside you and drop a little of the mixture in. If it forms into a ball it is ready.

Another way of testing is to use a traditional sugar thermometer, which has the temperatures and stages labeled on the side. The one you're looking for here is the "soft ball" stage. The most accurate method is to use a digital thermometer, and the temperature you need is between 239 and 244°F/115 and 118°C.

Keep mixing and, as soon as it's ready, take it off the heat, add the oat mixture immediately, and mix it all together really well. Keep mixing to cool and thicken it—this is the most strenuous bit—and you will know it is ready when your arms begin to hurt and the mixture is tighter and tougher to mix. It should start coming away from the sides of the pan. When it does, spoon the mixture into the prepared pan and use the back of a spoon to smooth and press it out evenly.

Let cool completely before cutting into small 1¼-inch/3cm squares. As they cool they will harden up. These store really well in an airtight jar. Flapjack or fudge or both—you decide!

chapter two

NO-BAKE BAKES

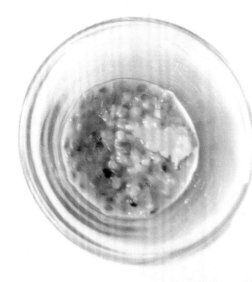

banana ice cream cheesecake with blueberry compote

For the base

vegetable oil or spray, for greasing

1¾ cups/160g rolled oats

mounded 1 cup/160g roasted whole hazelnuts

¼ cup/60ml coconut oil, + extra for the pan

½ cup/185g golden syrup or light corn syrup

a pinch of salt

For the filling

7 bananas, chopped and frozen

2 tablespoons golden syrup or light corn syrup

½ teaspoon ground cinnamon

1 tablespoon cocoa powder

For the compote

1½ cups/250g fresh or frozen blueberries

½ lemon, finely grated zest and juice

½ cup/100g granulated sugar

Serves 8–12   **Prep** 30 minutes, plus chilling and freezing   **Cook** 15 minutes

---

Cheesecake in any form is a winner for me and this is a simple no-bake ice cream version, which also happens to be vegan. Its sweet, oaty, nutty crust is filled with a banana "cheesecake" layer, then topped with a warm blueberry compote.

Start by lining and lightly greasing the bottom and sides of an 8-inch/20cm round removable-bottom pan, 3 inches/7.5cm deep.

Make the crust of the cheesecake by toasting the oats and the hazelnuts in a large frying pan on medium heat for about 5 minutes, until they just start to turn a golden brown, making sure to stir all the time to keep the oats moving. Pop them straight into a food processor and blitz to a fine crumb.

Now add the coconut oil, golden syrup, and salt and blitz again till it all clumps together.

Throw the mixture into the prepped pan and, using the back of a spoon, press into the bottom up 1 inch/2.5cm of the sides. Let the base chill while you make the filling.

Make the filling by taking out the frozen chopped bananas and putting in a food processor with the golden syrup, cinnamon, and cocoa. As tempted as you might be to begin whizzing, walk away for 5 minutes and allow the bananas to defrost just very slightly so that they process more easily, then blitz till you have what looks like a soft-serve ice cream.

Quickly spoon the mixture on top of the prepped crust and pop into the freezer till you are ready to eat.

When you are ready to eat, make the compote by combining the blueberries, lemon zest and juice, and sugar in a pan and stirring over medium heat till the blueberries have just softened. This should only take a few minutes. You can make the compote well in advance and, if you do, keep it chilled in the fridge until serving.

Take the cheesecake out of the freezer, slide it out of the cake pan, and put it onto your serving dish. Add the warm compote on top and let rest for just a few minutes before slicing and enjoying.

blueberry shinni cake

vegetable oil or spray, for greasing the pan

⅓ cup/50g dried blueberries

4 cups/500g all-purpose flour

1 teaspoon ground cinnamon

1 teaspoon ground green cardamom, pre-ground or grind yourself

½ teaspoon salt

1 cup + 2 tablespoons/ 250g unsalted butter, chopped into cubes

2 cups/480ml boiling water

1¼ cups/250g granulated sugar

2½ oz/75g white chocolate, melted

Serves 20 **Prep** 25 minutes, plus chilling **Cook** 10 minutes

Shinni is a Bengali spiced flour dough that is served during celebrations and tough times too. Nobody ever really makes it "just because," so I think that's the reason why I like making it a "just because"—for no particular reason besides a craving for something delicious. It's often served hot, ready for adults and children alike to pinch off warm mounds of the stuff from one large serving dish. But I quite enjoy it cooled, so I've come up with a way to serve it in exactly that fashion, cooked and cooled in a ring with a hidden surprise of dried blueberries that adorn the top when turned out, then drizzled with melted white chocolate.

Have a 10-inch/25cm Bundt pan (or just a springform cake pan) at the ready and grease well, or use a silicone cake pan. Put the blueberries into the bottom.

Toast the flour in a nonstick large wok or pot for 10 minutes on medium heat till golden brown. It's hard to see the change, so compare it to a bag of untoasted flour so you can see. Take off the heat and add the cinnamon, cardamom, and salt and stir well.

Add the butter, pop the pan back on the heat, and stir till you have a greasy flour and all the butter chunks are melted.

Measure out the 2 cups/480ml of boiling water into a pitcher or bowl, add the sugar, and stir till it is dissolved. Make a well in the center of the flour mixture and pour the hot sugary mix into the center. Using a whisk, bring the mixture together till you have a dough too tough to mix any more.

Take two spoons and scoop the dough into the Bundt pan on top of the blueberries, making sure to keep them where they are. Do this all the way around till you have filled the Bundt pan.

Pat and pack it all in, then let cool. When just slightly warm, refrigerate for at least 1 hour.

Turn out and drizzle all over with the melted white chocolate, then slice and eat.

tropical no-bake cookie one-pan cake

Serves up to 9   Prep 20 minutes

14 oz/400g chocolate shortbread cookies

1 cup/240ml whole milk

1 x 24-oz/700g jar of tropical fruit in juice, drained

1 lime, finely grated zest only

a small handful of fresh mint

2½ cups/600ml heavy cream

2 teaspoons almond extract

5 tablespoons/40g confectioners' sugar

¼ cup/20g toasted sliced almonds

This is the cheat of all cheats, with no actual baking involved, just a little bit of buying and putting together. It consists of cookies (chocolate shortbread, of course), soaked in milk, topped with almond cream, and adorned with tropical fruit out of a jar, then finished with the zing of some lime and mint, an extra helping of crushed cookies, and a scattering of toasted sliced almonds.

Have a 9 x 13-inch/23 x 33cm rectangular dish at the ready. I use a glass dish just because I like to see up the sides and all that's going on, but I'm nosy, so use what you have.

Line the bottom with the chocolate shortbread. You may need to break off bits of cookie to fill the little spaces that don't quite take whole cookies. Just do this till you have the bottom covered, saving any that are left over to crumble over the top.

Gently pour all your milk over the cookies and allow them to soften.

Now place the tropical fruit in a bowl. Add the lime zest and mint and mix well.

Put the cream in a bowl with the almond extract and confectioners' sugar and whip till the mixture comes to stiff peaks. Add to the top of the soaked cookies and spread over evenly. Scatter the fruity mix all over.

Place the remainder of the cookies in a bag and crush till you have uneven crumbs. Scatter all over along with the toasted almonds.

Pop in the fridge till you are ready to eat it.

strawberry and tarragon charlotte
with passion fruit

butter, for greasing
the pan

10 oz/275g Madeira
cake, store-bought or
homemade

5¼ oz/150g white
chocolate, melted

8 passion fruit, to serve

For the bavarois cream

1⅔ cups/400ml half-
and-half

2 x ¼-oz envelopes of
powdered gelatin

½ cup/100g granulated
sugar

6 large egg yolks

360g fresh or frozen
strawberries

a large handful of
fresh tarragon

Serves 8–10   **Prep** 35 minutes, plus chilling
Cook 15 minutes

I learned to make this many, many years ago. It has a bavarois cream in the middle, which is basically a custard set with gelatin that you can flavor with your choice of fruit purée and set in any sort of mold. I like mine encased in a cake dough, set, sliced, and served with passion fruit.

Line an 8½ x 4½-inch/900g loaf pan. Grease the inside first and then line with a layer of plastic wrap so the bottom and sides are covered, leaving some overhang.

Start by making the cake casing. Crumble the cake into a bowl till you have a fine crumb. Add the melted chocolate to the mixture and get your hands in till the mixture holds together when squeezed. Pop the mixture into the pan and, using your hands and the back of a spoon, press into the bottom of the pan and push the mixture up the sides, leaving a ¾-inch/2cm gap from the top. Put in the fridge and let chill while you make the bavarois.

For the bavarois, pour the half-and-half into a pot and sprinkle the powdered gelatin over the surface. Let stand for 5 to 10 minutes. Bring to a boil, stirring until dissolved, then take it off the heat.

Whisk together the sugar and egg yolks. Pour in the hot half-and-half slowly, then pour the mixture back into the pot and gently cook, stirring with a spatula, for 5 minutes on medium heat, till the mixture comes up to 176°F/80°C. Strain through a sieve to remove any lumps.

Blend the strawberries with the tarragon till they are mushed and strain through the same sieve into the hot custard mix. Get rid of the pulp and mix the smooth strawberry and tarragon into the custard.

Pour into the pan over the chilled cake lining and let chill in the fridge for up to 4 hours or overnight, till completely set. When you are ready to eat, take the pulp out of the passion fruit and serve with the sliced charlotte.

caramel crunch rocky road

Makes 12 squares
Prep 30 minutes, plus chilling
Cook 2 minutes

butter, for greasing the pan

8 x 1¾-oz/52g caramel-filled chocolates, ideally ones with cookie in

5¼ oz/150g dark chocolate, chopped or chips

¼ cup/50g unsalted butter

2 tablespoons golden syrup or light corn syrup

2½ oz/70g thin, crunchy Italian-style breadsticks, lightly broken

1 cup/150g pistachios, roughly chopped

a good pinch of sea salt flakes

For the white layer

5¼ oz/150g white chocolate, chopped or chips

¼ cup/50g unsalted butter

2 tablespoons golden syrup or light corn syrup

scant ½ cup/65g dried cherries and berries

½ cup/65g dried apricots, chopped

There are few rules where rocky road is concerned, but it must be chewy, crunchy, and gooey and, of course, contain lots of chocolate. This recipe has all of that and layers too! A gooey layer of chocolate-caramel sweets and melted chocolate mixed with breadsticks for a super-crispy crunch, then a layer of bright salted pistachios and finally a layer of sweet white chocolate mixed with chopped apricots and berries. All set and sliced and ready to indulge.

Begin by lining and lightly greasing a 7 x 10-inch/ 18 x 25cm rectangular cake pan or a 8-inch/20cm square cake pan.

Take the chocolates out of their wrappers and line them up on the bottom of the pan till you have no more spaces. It's okay to have some gaps; when you put on the next layer, it seeps through to hold it together.

Combine the dark chocolate, butter, and golden syrup in a microwaveable bowl and heat for 1 min- ute. Take out and mix till you have a smooth mixture. Let cool for 10 minutes. Add the breadsticks to the mixture and mix till well coated. Spread out evenly on top of the chocolates.

Now, sprinkle with the chopped pistachios until the bottom is covered all over. Use the back of a spoon to pat the mixture down and sprinkle with the sea salt flakes. Pop in the fridge for 30 minutes to set a little.

Make the white layer by putting the white chocolate, butter, and golden syrup in a microwaveable bowl and melting in the microwave for 1 minute. Take out and stir till smooth. If it looks like it is starting to sep- arate, add a little hot water one spoonful at a time, mixing after each addition till it comes back together and is smooth and glossy.

Add the cherries and berries and chopped apricots and mix well.

Take the pan out of the fridge and add the white layer, making sure to spread evenly, then pop back into the fridge to set for at least a few hours.

Take out and slice, then refrigerate until ready to eat.

scotch creme eggs

Serves 12   **Prep** 20 minutes, plus chilling

6 creme eggs

3¼ oz/90g oaty cookies

For the cakey coating

10½ oz/300g Madeira cake or pound cake, store-bought or homemade

1 lemon, finely grated zest only

3 tablespoons unsalted butter, softened

2 tablespoons confectioners' sugar, sifted

1 teaspoon whole milk

My husband and children love creme eggs, so I thought why not make something a little bit special with these to surprise them. I'm not usually a fan, but it turns out I can eat a creme egg happily when it's covered with zesty cake and coated in crumbs!

Start by removing the foil around the eggs, then put all six onto a plate and into the fridge.

Put the cookies into a freezer bag, seal, and crush using a rolling pin, or use a food processor, till you have really fine crumbs, then tip into a bowl.

Now for the cakey outer jacket. Take the cake and break the pieces into a bowl. Using your fingertips or a food processor, break up the cake till you have fine crumbs. Add the lemon zest.

Mix the butter, confectioners' sugar, and milk together to get a smooth buttercream. Add a spoon of cake crumbs at a time and mix using your hands so that you get a mixture that clumps together. Keep adding until it is easily moldable.

Divide the mixture into six and take the eggs out of the fridge. Take each cake mound and flatten in the palm of your hands. Add an egg in the center and use your hands to mold the cake around the creme egg, really packing the cake around it.

Add each mound to the bowl of biscuit crumbs and roll around till the crumbs coat the cake mixture.

Chill in the fridge till you are ready to eat. I like to allow them to chill fully so they're easier to cut in half. A half goes a very long way!

chewy chocolate krispy squares

<table>
<tr><td>½ cup/120g unsalted butter, + extra for greasing the pan</td><td>3 tablespoons/70g golden syrup or light corn syrup</td></tr>
<tr><td>6 x 1½ oz/40g nougat caramel chocolate bars, such as Milky Way, 4 chopped and 2 thinly sliced</td><td>¼ teaspoon salt
12 cups/300g puffed rice cereal</td></tr>
<tr><td></td><td>9 oz/250g milk chocolate, melted</td></tr>
</table>

Makes 16   **Prep** 15 minutes plus setting
Cook 10 minutes

These are like the chocolate rice crispy cakes we used to make at school. The kind that ended up in your mouth before they could even make it into the flimsy paper liners. These are delicious and chewy because they are made with chocolate bars already loaded with caramel and nougat. Sometimes simple and nostalgic is just what you need.

Start by lining the bottom and sides of an 8-inch/ 20cm square pan with parchment paper, making sure you have some overhang, then lightly grease.

Put the butter, chopped chocolate bars, golden syrup, and salt into a large heatproof bowl.

Part-fill a saucepan with some water. Bring the water to a boil and lower the heat. Put the bowl over the pan, making sure it sits comfortably without touching the water.

Gently mix till everything has melted and is an even, viscous layer. You may find you need to stir constantly to prevent the mixture from sticking to the bottom of the bowl. Take off the heat.

Put the puffed rice cereal in a large bowl with lots of room to mix and pour the chocolatey mixture right on top. Stir until every bit of cereal is totally coated.

Dump the lot into the lined pan and use the back of a greased spoon to level off the top.

Take the melted chocolate and spread it over the top in an even layer. Place your slices of chocolate bar all over and allow the chocolate to set in the fridge.

Cut into squares and you are ready to eat. Welcome to your childhood, but just less messy!

mango and black peppercorn cranachan

6 tablespoons/85g unsalted butter

2½ cups/100g corn flakes cereal

1 teaspoon ground black peppercorns

1 x 16-oz/450g can of mango pulp

1 small mango, peeled and chopped

2½ cups/600ml heavy cream

3 tablespoons granulated sugar

1 tablespoon confectioners' sugar

Makes 6   Prep 20 minutes   Cook 5 minutes

I love simple creamy desserts like this, which are easy to make, easy to adapt, and easy to prepare in advance. This is my slightly unorthodox take on a classic Scottish recipe, which traditionally contains cream, raspberries, and oats, but in my version the soft cream is swirled with mango and buttery corn flakes, with a hint of black peppercorns.

Start by cooking up those corn flakes. Heat the butter in a large nonstick pan and as soon as the butter is melted and hot, add the corn flakes.

Toast the corn flakes for about 5 minutes, till they are golden and have soaked up the butter. They need to be very crisp, toasty, and noisy, so just keep stirring and moving them around.

Pop the corn flakes onto a baking sheet, sprinkle with the black pepper and, using a spoon, toss them around so they all get a little bit of that black pepper.

Let cool.

Add the mango pulp to a bowl with the mango pieces, mix, and set aside.

Have six serving dishes at the ready and spoon a layer of the mango mixture into the bottom of each.

Put the cream in a bowl with the granulated sugar and whip to soft peaks. Now add a third of the cooled corn flakes and fold them in. Add the mango mixture, leaving just a little for the tops of all six, then ripple the mango through the cream. Add to the six dishes on top of the mango base.

Spoon the remaining mango on top. If you are ready to eat, add the remaining corn flakes; if not, chill and store the flakes in an airtight container till you are good and ready.

Serve the desserts with their crunchy top and dusted with a sprinkling of confectioners' sugar.

→

summer fruit tea-ramisu

7 oz/200g white chocolate, roughly chopped	2½ cups/350g frozen summer berries, defrosted and drained of any excess liquid
7 tablespoons/100ml hot water	1¾ oz/50g white chocolate, grated
1⅔ cups/400ml boiling water	**For the creamy filling**
6 English breakfast tea bags	4 large eggs
3 tablespoons granulated sugar	½ cup/100g granulated sugar
1 lemon, finely grated zest and juice	1 teaspoon vanilla extract
6 oz/175g ladyfingers	a pinch of salt
	3⅓ cups/750g mascarpone

Serves 12 **Prep** 40 minutes

This is a tiramisu but—as the name suggests—made with tea, rather than coffee, since that is my hot beverage of choice. (Coffee, to me, just tastes like airplane fuel!) So I steep my ladyfinger cookies in lemon-infused English breakfast tea and liven everything up with a layer of summer fruits.

This is the kind of recipe where you want to make up all the stages first and then assemble in one crack, so let's do that.

To start the tiramisu, put the chopped chocolate in a bowl, pour in the 7 tablespoons/100ml hot water, and mix till you have a smooth mixture. Set aside to cool. That's one bit done.

Meanwhile, prep the tea by putting the 1⅔ cups/ 400ml boiling water in a pitcher or bowl with the tea bags and sugar. Let the tea bags steep for 5 minutes, then squeeze out as much of that delicious darkness as possible. Take out the tea bags and add the juice and zest of the lemon. Set this aside too.

Now to make the creamy filling. I like to go back to basics and do this with a whisk, which allows more control and prevents the mascarpone from being overbeaten. Separate the eggs and put the yolks in a bowl with the granulated sugar and vanilla.

Put the whites into another clean bowl. Whisk the egg whites first with the pinch of salt till you have stiff peaks that hold.

Using the same whisk, go straight into the egg yolk bowl and whisk till you have a smooth, creamy mixture that is light and pale.

Now place the mascarpone in a smaller bowl and give it a quick mix to make it viscous and easier to mix in. Add the mascarpone to the egg yolk mixture and whisk till combined, then gently fold in the egg whites. Now you have all your elements ready to go.

Have a deep rectangular dish (about 9 x 13 inches/ 23 x 33cm and 3 quarts/2.7 liters) at the ready.

Take a ladyfinger and gently dunk it into the tea until it is fully immersed and soaked all over, then put it in the bottom of the dish. Do this one at a time till you have covered the entire bottom of the dish with soaked ladyfingers.

Take the chocolate mixture, pour half of it over the soaked ladyfingers, and spread evenly. Take one half of the summer fruits and sprinkle evenly all over the chocolate mixture. Now spoon in half of the mascarpone mixture and spread over the berries in an even layer.

Add another layer of the ladyfingers, dipping them one at a time into the tea till you have done all of them. Spread the rest of the white chocolate mix over the top and even the layer out. Add the rest of the summer fruits, then evenly top with the rest of the cream mixture.

Sprinkle with the grated chocolate and pop into the fridge overnight before serving. It needs to really set, so it's a perfect dessert to make in advance.

chocolate orange vegan mousse

Makes 6   **Prep** 40 minutes, plus soaking and chilling

For the cream

1 cup/150g cashews

1 teaspoon vanilla bean paste

1 teaspoon granulated sugar

¾ cup/175ml nut milk, + more as needed

For the mousse

chickpea water (aquafaba), drained from a 15-oz/400g can

½ cup/100g granulated sugar

3½ oz/100g dark chocolate, melted and cooled

1 teaspoon vanilla extract

2 oranges, finely grated zest only, keeping the rest for the topping

For the topping

3 oranges (2 from before + another)

2 large sprigs of fresh thyme

I'm not vegan but I try to reduce my meat and dairy consumption where I can, so I like experimenting with vegan versions of all kinds of recipes. I've discovered some wonderful alternatives, including this mousse, which is made using chickpea water, known as aquafaba. A good vegan recipe should make you forget about the ingredients that are not included because you're too busy enjoying the ones in front of you. Chocolate, orange, and a hint of thyme—what's not to love?

Put the cashews in a bowl and pour in boiling water till the nuts are covered. Let soak for 1 hour.

For the mousse, put the liquid from the chickpeas in a bowl. This will become the base of your mousse. As with any meringue, ensure the bowl is grease-free or it could prevent the chickpea water from whisking up.

Using electric beaters or a stand mixer, whisk for about 8 to 10 minutes, till the mixture is light and fluffy. Now add the sugar a spoonful at a time, allowing it enough time to dissolve after each addition. You need to whisk for longer with each addition of sugar than you would if making meringue with egg whites, but this stuff is amazing because, unlike with egg whites, you can't overdo it, so keep whisking to stiff peaks.

As soon as you can hold the bowl over your head without the whites falling out, add the melted dark chocolate and fold it in. Then add the vanilla and orange zest and fold in till you have a smooth mixture. You will lose some volume in your mousse, but that is to be expected. Spoon the mixture into six jam jars or glasses and pop into the fridge.

Drain the nuts and pop into a blender. Add the vanilla, granulated sugar, and ¾ cup/175ml of nut milk and whiz till you have a smooth, thick, cream-like consistency. Add a splash more milk if it is very thick. Pour straight onto the top of the mousse in all six jars. Pop into the fridge and prep the fruit.

Top and tail the oranges, cut off all the peel, and remove each segment. Chop the segments into pieces and mix with the thyme leaves.

When you are ready to eat, serve the mousses with the orange segments on top.

virgin mojito possets

Makes 6   Prep 25 minutes, plus chilling
Cook 10 minutes

For the apples

1 green apple, peeled, cored, and diced

1 lime, juice only

a small handful of fresh mint leaves, finely chopped

For the posset

2½ cups/600ml heavy cream

¾ cup/140g granulated sugar

5 juicy limes, juice and finely grated zest

For the crunchy apple topping

1 green apple, grated, excess moisture squeezed out

1 tablespoon coconut oil, melted

½ teaspoon ground ginger

1 teaspoon confectioners' sugar

I drink "virgin" everything. Mocktails have become very popular with millennials and, while I'm not sure I quite count as a millennial, it feels great to be a part of an "in" group. I love virgin mojitos, with their combination of fresh apple and mint and a hint of citrus, and if I'm feeling like I want a real hit, I occasionally make them with ginger ale instead of lemonade—that is as wild as I get! This recipe takes all those fresh flavors and puts them into a creamy posset.

Start with six ramekins, about 7 oz/200ml each. Take your diced apple and pop into a bowl with the lime juice. This is for sharpness and will prevent the apple from browning too. Add the mint to the bowl and mix. Divide the mixture among the ramekins.

Now make the posset by combining the cream in a saucepan with the sugar and mixing so the sugar dissolves and mixes into the cream. Put the mixture onto high heat and bring to a boil, stirring occasionally. Lower the heat as soon as it does and let simmer for just 3 minutes.

Take off the heat, add the lime juice and zest, and stir well. The mixture should start to thicken almost as soon as you add the lime and mix. Gently pour into the ramekins on top of the apples and let cool just slightly before popping into the fridge. These need at least 3 hours to set. The apple pieces will float up to the top, but you can't keep a good thing down!

Meanwhile, make the easy crunchy apple topping. Have a large plate ready, lined with some parchment paper. Mix the grated apple with the coconut oil and spread evenly all over the lined plate. Pop in the microwave for 2 minutes on the highest setting and then for 20-second bursts till you have very crisp, dry grated apple. Between each bout in the microwave, give the apple shreds a little stir to move them around and also to check that they are crisping up. Once they are crisp, sprinkle with the ground ginger and confectioners' sugar and mix well.

Once your possets are set, crumble the apple over the top and they are ready to eat.

strawberry rice pudding fool

Serves 6 **Prep** 20 minutes, plus soaking
Cook 25 minutes

The inspiration for this came a few years ago, when we took our kids to Disney World, and we had a meal among make-believe princesses. Yet all I can remember is the pudding. Ever since then I've wanted to return, not for the princesses but for the dessert. I finally decided to make it myself. Now, mine could be totally different, but it tastes divine. Crushed rice cooked, cooled, and whipped through cream, and then marbled with strawberry coulis, which I've kept chunky, scented with lime zest and cardamom. Yum!

Begin by putting the rice into a bowl or pitcher. Add the water and milk and let soak for just 10 minutes. I use an immersion blender, so I like to put the mixture into the tall container that came with the blender, or you can save on washing up by doing this in your food processor. Once the 10 minutes are up, whiz with the blender or processor in short bursts till the rice has broken up into bits.

For the rice pudding

- 6 tablespoons/75g basmati rice
- ¾ cup + 2 tablespoons/ 200ml cold water
- 7 tablespoons/100ml whole milk
- 1 vanilla pod, seeds removed
- ¼ cup/50g granulated sugar
- 2½ cups/600ml heavy cream

For the strawberry coulis

- 1 pound/450g strawberries, chopping 8 oz/225g into small cubes
- 6 cardamom pods, seeds removed
- 3 limes, finely grated zest only
- 1½ tablespoons confectioners' sugar

Pour the mixture into a small saucepan, add the vanilla seeds and granulated sugar, and pop onto high heat. Bring to a boil, making sure to stir all the time, and, as soon as it comes to a boil, decrease to very low heat and cook for 20 to 25 minutes, stirring constantly, until the rice is mostly soft with a little bite to it but no grittiness. As soon as the rice grains are cooked, take off the heat, pop into a bowl, and spread out to allow it to cool as fast as possible.

Now on to the coulis. Put the whole strawberries in a bowl along with the cardamom seeds, lime zest, and confectioners' sugar and blitz to a smooth, delicious sauce. Add the chopped strawberries, mix, and set aside.

When the rice has cooled, add 7 tablespoons/100ml of the cream and stir in well to loosen. Now pour the rest of the cream into a bowl and whisk till you have soft peaks—this should not take long. Add the rice to the cream and fold it in till you have an even mixture.

Add two-thirds of the strawberry mixture in dollops onto the rice and gently fold it in to create ripples. Spoon into a large serving dish or six individual dishes and top with the leftover coulis.

chapter three

TARTS
& PIES

—

carrot tart

Serves 8   Prep 30 minutes, plus chilling
Cook 50 minutes

For the crust

4½ oz/125g graham crackers

scant ¼ cup/25g whole hazelnuts

¼ cup/50g unsalted butter, melted

1½ tablespoons golden syrup or light corn syrup

a pinch of salt

For the carrot filling

14 oz/400g carrots, grated

1 tablespoon butter

1 tablespoon water

5 tablespoons/60g granulated sugar

a pinch of salt

1 teaspoon ground cinnamon

1 teaspoon whole coriander seeds, crushed

2 large eggs

2 tablespoons unsalted butter

3 tablespoons milk

To serve

whipped cream

chopped hazelnuts

This is my take on a pumpkin pie, but made with carrots because I always have loads in the fridge and this is a great way to use them up. Just like the original, it has a beautiful vibrant orange color. Spiced with crushed coriander and cinnamon, the filling is baked in a crumbly cookie and hazelnut crust. If you prefer to make this with pumpkin, just swap the main ingredient like for like, though it's best to remove the skin.

Preheat the oven to 350°F and have a 10-inch/25cm fluted pie dish at the ready.

Start by making the crust. Pop the graham crackers into a food processor along with the hazelnuts and blitz to a fine crumb. Now add the melted butter, golden syrup, and salt and blitz till you have a mixture that resembles wet sand. Pour out all the mixture into the pie dish. Using the back of a spoon, push the mixture into the bottom and sides till you have an even layer all over.

Get a piece of parchment paper that will fit inside the crust-lined dish and scrunch it up (this just makes it easier to shape). Put on top of the graham cracker crust and fill with baking beads.

Bake in the oven for 20 minutes.

Meanwhile, start the filling by putting the carrots in a bowl with the butter and water and covering tightly with some plastic wrap. Pop into a microwave and cook on the highest setting for 10 minutes. Being careful because the bowl will be very hot, take out and take the plastic wrap off, then let cool for 10 minutes.

As soon as the crust is done, take out of the oven. Lower the oven temperature to 325°F. Remove the paper and baking beads.

Now back to the filling. Put the cooked carrot into the food processor and add the granulated sugar, salt, cinnamon, and coriander seeds. Blitz smooth, then add the eggs, butter, and milk and give it a final whiz.

Pour the mixture straight onto the baked crust and bake for 30 minutes. If after 20 minutes you find the edges are starting to catch or get dark, pop a piece of foil on top for the rest of the baking time. Once baked, take out of the oven and let cool completely. Once it is totally cooled, I recommend chilling it for at least 3 hours before you eat it.

Serve chilled, with whipped cream and a sprinkling of hazelnuts. It will keep in the fridge for 3 days.

portuguese custard tarts

For the tart shells

13 oz/375g pre-rolled puff pastry

1 teaspoon ground nutmeg

For the filling

¾ cup/155g granulated sugar

1 large egg

2 large egg yolks

1 tablespoon cornstarch

1 teaspoon vanilla extract

1⅔ cups/400ml heavy cream

a pinch of ground nutmeg

Makes 12   **Prep** 30 minutes, plus cooling
Cook 35 minutes

The first time I ate these was out of a box from the local supermarket. Second time was at a popular chain restaurant. Third time was at a food market in London. They got slightly better each time, but then I had them in Portugal, in the sun, and that's when I really had them. The crisp, buttery tart shell is filled with a set custard with just a kiss of nutmeg. Delicious! Easy to eat, but really easy to make too, especially if you want to get close to the real thing.

Start by sorting the pastry. Roll the pastry out and sprinkle the dough evenly with the nutmeg.

Now roll up the pastry like you would a cinnamon bun, starting with the long edge, until the whole thing is fully rolled up. Cut into 12 equal pieces.

Have a 12-hole muffin pan at the ready. Pop each round of pastry into one of the cups of the pan, with the swirly side up so you can see the swirls of nutmeg.

Dampen your hands slightly so the pastry doesn't stick and, using your thumbs, push the pastry from the center out so the dough evenly covers the bottom and all the way up the sides of each cup. Pop into the fridge while you make the custard.

Start on the custard by combining the sugar, egg, egg yolks, cornstarch, and vanilla in a bowl and whisk till combined.

Put the cream into a pot and just bring to a boil. As soon as it comes up to a boil, take off the heat. Gently pour the hot cream in a very steady stream into the eggy mixture.

Pour it all back into the pot and heat gently, stirring all the time till the mixture has thickened. As soon as it has, take off the heat. Let cool for 30 minutes.

Preheat the oven to 400°F.

Take the pastry out of the fridge and pour the custard mixture into the pastry, leaving a slight gap on top just to make sure they are not overfilled. Sprinkle a dusting of nutmeg on the top of each one.

Pop into the oven and bake for 20 to 25 minutes. The custard filling will puff up over the edges, but don't worry, because as soon as they come out of the oven and begin to cool, they come right back down.

I would let these rest for about 30 minutes so the custard is fully set before eating. However, they are equally delicious chilled out of the fridge. It all depends on your patience and/or desperation!

grapefruit ganache tart

Serves 8–10
Prep 45 minutes, plus chilling **Cook** 35 minutes

For the pastry

1¼ cups/160g all-purpose flour

¼ cup/ 20g cocoa powder

5 tablespoons/40g confectioners' sugar

a pinch of salt

½ cup/110g cold unsalted butter, cubed

1 large egg yolk

For the filling

10½ oz/300g white chocolate, chopped or chips

¾ cup + 2 tablespoons/ 200ml heavy cream

1 grapefruit, finely grated zest only (saving the juice for the sauce)

For the sauce

juice of 1 grapefruit (approx. ¾ cup + 2 tablespoons/ 200ml)

6 tablespoons/75g granulated sugar

¼ cup/50g unsalted butter

1 teaspoon cornstarch

This has all the qualities of a great tart plus some bonus features. The short, crumbly pastry crust contains cocoa, which makes it a beautiful dark color. The rich, velvety ganache filling is offset with a hint of grapefruit. It's served with a zesty grapefruit sauce drizzled all over.

For the pastry, put the dry ingredients in a food processor. Add the butter and blitz till you have a fine breadcrumb-like texture. Add the egg yolk and blitz again till you get clumps gathering and no excess flour. If it is too floury and not coming together, add a few drops of water and whiz till small clumps start to form.

Now tip the dough clumps out and bring together into a nice round mound. Flatten and wrap in plastic wrap. Pop into the fridge to chill for 30 minutes.

Meanwhile, preheat the oven to 400°F and put a baking sheet on the middle shelf. Have a 9-inch/23cm fluted removable-bottomed pan at the ready.

Take out the pastry and on a floured surface roll out to about 14 inches/35cm diameter—large enough to line the base and sides of the pan with an overhang.

Line the pan with the pastry, making sure to get it into the edges. Prick the base with a fork to make holes for steam to escape. Put in the freezer for 15 minutes.

Take out and fill the crust with parchment paper and baking beads. Blind bake for 15 minutes, then remove the paper and beads, and bake for 10 minutes. Take out and let cool 10 minutes before carefully cutting off any overhanging pastry.

Allow the tart crust to cool in the pan and start on the filling by putting the chocolate in a heatproof bowl.

Pour the cream into a small pot and gently heat. As soon as the cream just comes to a boil, take off the heat and pour straight into the chocolate. Stir until it has all mixed in, the chocolate has melted, and the mixture is smooth. Add the zest of the grapefruit and stir well, then pour into the prepared tart shell. Pop into the fridge and let chill completely.

Make the sauce by combining the juice, sugar, butter, and cornstarch in a small pot. Pop onto low to medium heat and mix till it is smooth and thick and coats the back of the spoon. Take off the heat.

Once the tart is chilled, slice, plate, drizzle, and enjoy. This will keep in the fridge for 3 days.

french onion and blue cheese tart

2 tablespoons butter

2 large sprigs of lemon thyme

1 clove of garlic, grated

5 onions, thinly sliced (you will need about 2 pounds 2 oz/1kg)

1 teaspoon freshly ground black pepper

1 teaspoon salt

2 teaspoons granulated sugar

1 sheet of pre-rolled puff pastry

1 egg, lightly beaten

5¼ oz/150g blue cheese

a small handful of chopped fresh chives, to serve

> **Serves** 8 **Prep** 25 minutes
> **Cook** 45 minutes

Given how often we need onions to start a recipe, let's not forget or discount how important they really are. So in this tart I've made them the star of the show, sweet and lightly scented, in pride of place on a layer of light, puffy pastry and delicious crumbled blue cheese.

Start by cooking the onions. They need to be cooked slowly on low heat, so it's best to begin with those.

Melt the butter in a large nonstick frying pan—we have a load of onions to cook. When the butter has melted, pick off the thyme leaves and add, then add the garlic and onions. Mix everything together.

Now add the pepper, salt, and sugar and mix. Cook on medium heat for 30 minutes, stirring occasionally, until you have onions that look like the kind you would only eat with a burger in a Sunday market at 6 a.m.!

While that cooks, start on the pastry. Preheat the oven to 400°F. Line a baking sheet with some parchment paper or use the paper the pastry comes in and roll out the pastry onto the sheet.

Using a knife, score a smaller rectangle ½ inch/1cm inside the pastry rectangle, making sure not to cut all the way through. Pierce the inner rectangle with a fork all over to allow the steam to escape when it bakes.

Brush the edges with the egg and bake for 20 minutes, until golden all over.

Take out and, using the back of a spoon, push down all the puffed-up pastry of the inner rectangle, creating a nice neat border.

Take the blue cheese and crumble all over the inner rectangle of the pastry. Add the onions and scatter them all over till you have an even layer. Now bake for 15 minutes.

Take out and let cool for 10 minutes before eating, sprinkled with the chives.

orange and lemongrass meringue pie

Serves 8   Prep 30 minutes, plus chilling
Cook 10 minutes

For the crust

6 cups/250g sugar-frosted corn flake cereal

½ cup + 1 tablespoon/125g unsalted butter, melted

For the filling

2 large oranges, finely grated zest and squeezed juice (you will need ¾ cup + 2 tablespoons/200ml juice)

4 stalks of lemongrass

¼ cup/25g cornstarch

1¼ cups/250g granulated sugar

6 large egg yolks

For the meringue

4 large egg whites

½ teaspoon cream of tartar

1¼ cups/255g granulated sugar

½ cup/120ml water

Meringue pie is a classic, especially the familiar lemon variety. But it's also a recipe where there are so many variations possible, and this is just one of countless ways to mix it up. Instead of cookie crumbs or pastry, I've made the crust with sweet crisp cereal. And instead of lemon curd, I've gone for orange and lemongrass.

Line the bottom of a 9-inch/23cm removable-bottomed pan with a circle of parchment paper.

Pop the frosted flakes into a food processor and blitz to a fine crumb. You might need to do this in batches. Add the melted butter and whiz till you have a mixture that resembles wet, clumpy sand. Tip it out into the pan and, using the back of a spoon, cover the bottom and sides, making sure to pack it all in really tightly. Pop into the fridge to chill and set.

Now for the curd. Combine the orange zest and juice in a nonstick pot. Bash the lemongrass to release all the flavors, chop into little pieces, and add to the pot.

Add the cornstarch, sugar, and egg yolks and stir everything together. It will be lumpy and not look great at this point, but pop it onto the stove on the lowest heat and mix till you have a smooth curd that coats the back of a spoon.

Take off the heat and push through a fine-mesh sieve to remove lumps and extract more of that lemongrass flavor. Let cool completely. As soon as it is cool, add to the crispy tart crust, level the top, and pop into the fridge.

Put the egg whites and cream of tartar into the bowl of a stand mixer with the whisk attachment.

Mix the sugar and water in a medium saucepan. Heat gently until the sugar has dissolved, then bubble until the syrup reaches 230°F/110°C. When that happens, start beating the egg whites in the stand mixer until they reach stiff peaks. Once the syrup reaches 244°F/118°C, pour the syrup slowly onto the egg whites with the motor still running at low speed. Once the syrup is mixed in, increase the speed to medium–high and beat for another 3 to 5 minutes, until thick and shiny.

Take the tart crust out of the pan and put on a serving dish. Dollop peaks of meringue onto the curd. The more swirls you have the more beautiful it will look. Any leftover meringue can be dolloped on toast, as my children often do. Broil the top for just long enough to toast or use a blowtorch to color the meringue.

→

pecan pie empanadas

For the pastry

4½ cups/550g all-purpose flour

1 teaspoon salt

1 cup/230g unsalted butter

1 large egg + 1 large egg yolk, lightly beaten

½ cup + 1 tablespoon/ 140ml cold water

For the filling

2 large eggs

¼ cup/50g light brown sugar

½ cup + 2 tablespoons/ 150g unsalted butter, softened

3 tablespoons all-purpose flour

1 tablespoon whole milk

1 teaspoon vanilla extract

2 cups/200g pecans, roughly chopped

1 x 8-oz/227g jar of clotted cream or crème fraîche

1 egg, lightly beaten

vegetable oil, for frying

salt

Makes 26 **Prep** 50 minutes, plus chilling **Cook** 40 minutes **Can be assembled** a day in advance and then fried to serve

---

These are all-to-yourself pecan pies made in individual pastry parcels, so no sharing, just yours, to pick up and enjoy. Delicious crisp pastry is filled with a pecan and brown sugar mixture and, to make them even more delicious, clotted cream, like a built-in topping. As the empanadas fry and the filling warms up, so does the cream.

Start by making the pastry. Combine the flour and salt in a bowl and mix. Add the butter and rub in till you have something that resembles breadcrumbs.

Make a well in the center, add the eggs, and mix in. Add the water and mix till you have a dough that comes together in a mound. To make life easier you can do all of the above in a food processor in the same order till you have a dough. Flatten the dough, wrap in plastic wrap, and chill in the fridge for 1 hour to firm up.

Make the filling by combining the eggs, sugar, butter, flour, milk, vanilla, and pecans in a bowl and mixing till you have an even mixture. Set aside.

Roll the dough to about ⅛ inch/3mm thick, then cut out 26 circles with a 4-inch/10cm cutter. Spread the circles out on a surface and evenly distribute your filling onto them, making sure to put the filling off-center, because the other half has to fold over. Now add a small spoonful of cream on top.

Brush the unfilled half of each circle with beaten egg and fold over to enclose the filling. Press and seal all the way around the join. Pop them all onto a baking sheet and chill for 1 hour.

Heat enough oil in a pot to be able to shallow fry these. I like to use a large, deep frying pan and add enough oil to get just about halfway up. Heat the oil until, when you add a pinch of bread, it comes up to the surface. If you are using a thermometer, which is the most accurate way, then it needs to be at 356°F/180°C.

Add 3 or 4 empanadas, depending on the size of your pan, and fry for just a few minutes on each side till light golden brown. Each batch will take about 5 minutes. Sprinkle with a little salt as they come out of the oil and drain on paper towels. These are best eaten while hot.

canadian butter tart

Serves 8   Prep 25 minutes, plus cooling
Cook 1 hour

For the crust

butter or oil, for greasing the pan

1 pound 2 oz/500g store-bought piecrust dough, chopped into ½-inch/1cm chunks

¼ cup/30g confectioners' sugar, + extra for dusting

For the topping

2 large eggs

½ cup + 1 tablespoon/ 120g brown sugar

1 teaspoon almond extract

2 teaspoons instant coffee

1 tablespoon cornstarch

¼ cup/50g unsalted butter, melted

a pinch of salt

3 tablespoons whole milk

½ cup/50g walnuts, roughly chopped

⅔ cup/100g raisins or currants

This was a must-try item on my list of "things to eat" when we visited Canada one summer. Every bit of research I did told me to go and find these. They are sweet, crunchy with nuts, and crumbly with pastry. What I loved most about them was the pastry, as I always like more of it rather than less. So my version of the recipe has lots of chunky pastry pieces on the crust, and just a little of the sweetness with the buttery, nutty topping, plus raisins and a hint of coffee.

Preheat the oven to 400°F. Grease and line the bottom and sides of a square 8½-inch/22cm baking pan. Make sure to grease the inside on top of the parchment paper lightly too.

Take your chunks of pie dough, pop them into a bowl, and sprinkle with all of the confectioners' sugar. Toss around to make sure they are evenly coated with the sugar. Tip the pieces into the prepared pan in an even layer and sprinkle in any leftover sugar. Bake in the oven for about 30 minutes.

Meanwhile, make the topping by combining the eggs, brown sugar, almond extract, instant coffee, and cornstarch in a small nonstick saucepan and give it all a really good mix. Add the melted butter, salt, and milk and whisk till well combined.

Pop onto medium heat and keep whisking, heating the mixture till it becomes thicker. This should take 5 minutes. As soon as it has thickened, take off the heat, add the walnuts and raisins or currants and mix well.

Take the pastry crust out of the oven and top with the sweet butter mixture in an even layer. Pop back into the oven for 15 minutes. It will begin to bubble around the edges. Take out and let cool in the pan for 10 minutes.

Lift out and let rest on the paper on a cooling rack till totally cooled down. Cut out squares and dust with a little confectioners' sugar before serving.

potato rösti quiche

Serves 6   **Prep** 30 minutes, plus cooling **Cook** 50 minutes

For the base

butter or oil, for greasing the pan

1 large white potato, unpeeled (you should have 11½ oz/325g)

1 large sweet potato, unpeeled (you should have about 11½ oz/ 325g)

1 teaspoon salt

1 teaspoon paprika

1 teaspoon granulated garlic

1 tablespoon granulated onion

⅓ cup/40g all-purpose flour

1 large egg, + 1 beaten egg for brushing

For the filling

3 large eggs

½ cup + 2 tablespoons/ 150ml whole milk

5¼ oz/150g mature Cheddar cheese, grated

a small handful of fresh chives

salt and pepper

This re-imagined quiche is all about the crust! Made from different colored potatoes, grated and pressed into a pan, it's filled with a creamy cheese and chive mixture. Delicious and also super simple.

Preheat the oven to 350°F. Start by generously greasing a 9½-inch/24cm round tart pan or pie dish, preferably not removable-bottomed as this will save us from any leakages.

Grate the potatoes and squeeze out any excess moisture. Pop the potato into a bowl along with the salt, paprika, garlic, onion, and flour and mix really well, making sure it is all evenly distributed. Add the egg and mix well—you should have a mixture that is well coated and clumps together.

Tip the mixture out into the dish and, using the back of a spoon, press tightly into the bottom and sides. Bake for 25 to 30 minutes.

Take the dish out and, using the back of a spoon, press the mixture into the bottom and sides again. Brush the bottom and sides with the beaten egg, generously filling in any gaps that might be there and any gaps that might not be. More is more! Pop back into the oven for 5 minutes.

Meanwhile, make the filling by mixing the eggs and milk in a bowl and whisking till well blended.

Take the tart crust out and scatter the cheese over the crust. Pour the egg and milk mixture straight in, sprinkle with the chives, and add a sprinkling of salt and a generous sprinkling of pepper. Bake in the oven for 20 minutes, till the center is just wobbly.

Let cool for about 30 minutes, allowing the eggy custard mix to set, then take out, slice, and it is ready to eat.

sfeeha triangle

Serves 6-8
Prep 50 minutes, plus rising
Cook 55 minutes

For the dough

4 cups/500g bread flour, + extra for dusting

1 package (2¼ teaspoons/7g) fast-acting dried yeast

1 teaspoon granulated sugar

3 tablespoons olive oil

1 teaspoon salt

1¼ cups/300ml warm water

For the filling

3 tablespoons olive oil

3 cloves of garlic, crushed

¾ cup/100g pine nuts

1 small yellow onion, finely chopped

1 pound 2 oz/500g ground lamb

1 teaspoon salt

1 teaspoon cayenne pepper

1 tablespoon freshly ground black pepper

½ teaspoon ground cinnamon

1 teaspoon allspice

1 tablespoon honey

a large handful of fresh parsley

For the dip

½ cup + 2 tablespoons/ 150ml good olive oil

6 tablespoons/85g plain yogurt

a drizzle of pomegranate molasses

a handful of pomegranate seeds

1 teaspoon za'atar

For the glaze

¼ cup/50g unsalted butter, melted

a good pinch of salt

1 tablespoon dried parsley

I first ate this while fasting. We'd been to prayer, and afterward there was food on sale to raise money for charity. So my memories are doubly good, because as well as the wonderful feeling of giving, it's a little bit special when you get to break your fast and enjoy some food. The ones I ate that time were delicious little individual triangles, encasing a sweet, spicy ground meat filling, but my recipe is for one big triangle to share.

For the dough, put the flour in a large mixing bowl. Add the yeast, sugar, and oil to one side and the salt to the other side. Mix everything together and make a well in the center.

Add the water and mix till you bring the dough together. If you are using a mixer, knead with a dough hook attached, or lightly dust the work surface and knead the dough till it is smooth, pliable, and stretchy. This can take 10 minutes by hand or 5 minutes in a stand mixer. Pop back into the bowl, cover, and let rise in a warm place to double in size.

Meanwhile, make the filling. Warm the oil in a non-stick pan over medium heat. As soon as the oil is hot, add the garlic and pine nuts and, as soon as both are golden brown, add the onion and stir and cook for 10 minutes, till the onion is soft. Add the ground lamb and cook until browned.

Now add the salt, cayenne, black pepper, cinnamon, allspice, and honey. Cook for 10 minutes. Take off the heat, add all the parsley, and let cool completely.

Preheat the oven to 425°F and line a baking sheet with some parchment paper.

Once the dough has doubled in size, tip it out and knock out all the air. Roll the dough out to a circle that is about ¼ inch/5mm thin. Lift the dough onto the lined sheet.

Tip the mixture for the filling into the center of the dough in a circle. Now take the dough at three

equidistant points and bring right into the center so you have a triangle shape. Pinch in the center, but leave the seams on top exposed so you can see the filling. Push gently to flatten. Bake for 25 minutes.

To make the dip, pour the oil into a bowl and spoon the yogurt into the center. Drizzle with the pome-granate molasses, sprinkle on the pomegranate seeds and then the za'atar, and it's ready to devour.

Once the triangle is baked and while still hot, brush with the melted butter and sprinkle all over with the salt and dried parsley. Serve with the dip.

rainbow veg pakora picnic pie

For the filling

1 red bell pepper, diced

1 carrot, grated

1⅔ cups/285g corn kernels

1 small zucchini, diced

½ small eggplant, diced

½ small red onion, diced

a large handful of fresh chives, finely chopped

a large handful of fresh cilantro, finely chopped

1 teaspoon salt

2 teaspoons granulated garlic

2 teaspoons chile flakes

2 teaspoons cumin seeds

1 tablespoon curry powder, mild or hot, whatever you prefer

2 large eggs

1 cup/100g chickpea flour

For the pastry

2 cups + 2 tablespoons/265g all-purpose flour

½ cup/55g bread flour

½ teaspoon salt

2 teaspoons curry powder

½ cup + 1 tablespoon/135ml water

5 tablespoons/70g unsalted butter

1 egg, lightly beaten

Serves 8	Prep 1 hour
Cook 40 minutes	

Pies are the thing I find most satisfying to make and that doesn't even include the eating process! An all-in-one meal, in an edible casing, filled with pretty much anything you want (apart from soup! Let's not go there). This one is filled with lightly spiced rainbow veg, encased in a golden brown, curry-flavored pastry crust. Inspired by a pakora, it has all the colors, all of the flavor, but none of the frying.

Start by making the filling. Combine the red bell pepper, carrot, corn, zucchini, eggplant, onion, chives, and cilantro in a bowl. Add the salt, garlic, chile, cumin, and curry powder and get in there and mix till everything looks relatively evenly distributed.

Now add the eggs and mix well, then the flour and mix again. Set aside and get on to the pastry.

Preheat the oven to 400°F and have ready a 10-inch/25cm round tart pan, 2 inches/5cm deep and with a removable bottom or fixed bottom.

To make the pastry, combine the flours, salt, and curry powder in a bowl, mix, and create a small well in the center.

Warm the water in a small pot with the butter and bring to a boil. As soon as the butter has melted, take off the heat and add straight into the dry ingredients.

Mix using the back of a spoon and then, as soon as it is cool enough to handle, get your hands in and bring the dough together. When it does, divide the mixture by separating off one third.

Take the bigger bit and roll till you have pastry large enough to cover the bottom and sides of the pan with a little overhang.

Tip in the vegetable mixture and level the surface. Take the other bit of dough and roll till you have enough to cover the top. Brush the edge with egg and pop the top on. Trim the edges and then crimp. Cut a hole in the center for the air to escape. Brush the top with egg. Bake in the oven for 40 minutes.

Take out and let cool for at least 1 hour before eating.

beet tatin
with mackerel and a dill pesto

Serves 4   **Prep** 30 minutes   **Cook** 40 minutes

For the tatin

1 pound 2 oz/500g puff pastry block or pre-rolled puff pastry

3 tablespoons vegetable oil

14 oz/400g cooked beets, drained, dried, and quartered

2 tablespoons balsamic vinegar

2 tablespoons brown sugar

1 small orange, finely grated zest and juice

For the pesto

⅓ cup + 1 tablespoon/ 50g pine nuts, toasted

2 cloves of garlic

3½ oz/100g fresh dill, roughly chopped

½ cup/50g grated Parmesan cheese

½ cup + 2 tablespoons/ 150ml olive oil

To serve

5 oz/140g hot smoked mackerel, skin removed and flaked

crème fraîche

This is such a simple lunch or dinner and can easily be assembled in advance, ready to bake at a later point. I love beet, in particular the sheer purple of the veg, but also that sweet, delicious, earthy flavor, which I adore cooked gently with orange and covered with a flaky puff pastry. I like to serve this tart with flakes of hot smoked mackerel and a dill pesto. If you have pesto left over, store it in a jar covered with a thin layer of oil, then seal the lid and it will keep in the fridge for 1 to 2 weeks.

Preheat the oven to 400°F. For this recipe you need an oven-safe, round, deep frying pan, about 10 inches/ 25cm in diameter.

Roll the pastry into an 11½-inch/29cm circle. Pop onto a baking sheet and let chill.

Pour the oil in the pan and heat, then add the beets and warm through. These are already cooked, so half the work is done for you. Add the balsamic vinegar to the beets along with the sugar, orange juice, and zest and cook till the beets are coated in a thick, sticky mixture. This should take about 5 minutes, but be sure not to burn the sugar, and keep an eye on that. Take off the heat.

Bring the pastry out of the fridge and gently lay it on top of the beets.

Using a spatula or the end of a dinner knife, tuck the edges of the pastry into the pan under the beets. Do this all the way around to create a "cup," which will hold the beets once the tart is turned out. Pierce the top of the pastry to allow the steam to escape. Bake in the oven for 35 minutes.

Make the pesto by combining all the ingredients in a blender and whizzing till smooth.

When the tatin is ready, remove from the oven but let cool in the pan for 5 minutes before turning out. Turn out and add the flaked mackerel all over the top, then drizzle with the pesto and serve sliced with crème fraîche on the side.

chicken, brie, cranberry, and pink pepper pithivier

Serves 6   Prep 30 minutes, plus chilling
Cook 50 minutes   Can be assembled up to
1 day in advance and then baked to serve

2 x 1 pound 2 oz/500g blocks of puff pastry

all-purpose flour, for dusting

3 tablespoons olive oil

4 cloves of garlic

1 onion

1 teaspoon salt

¼ cup/35g pink peppercorns, crushed

10½ oz/300g boneless chicken thighs, cut into cubes

scant 1 cup/100g dried cranberries

2 egg yolks, lightly beaten

7 oz/200g Brie cheese

A French classic, this beautifully scored, round puff pastry pie can be filled with all manner of ingredients, sweet or savory. With such a reliable exterior, the inside is all to play for. I've filled mine with chicken that's spiced and sweetened with pink peppercorns and cranberries, around a delicious center of melted Brie.

Line two baking sheets with parchment paper.

Take the puff pastry blocks and roll them one by one on a floured surface. Roll to a ¼-inch/5mm thickness and cut using a 10-inch/25cm round, then cut another circle to a 12-inch/30cm round. Allow both to chill on a baking sheet while you make the filling.

Now make the filling by warming the oil in a large nonstick pan over medium heat. Blitz the garlic and onion in a food processor to a smooth paste.

Add the paste to the hot oil and cook till the mixture is thick and brown—this should take about 10 minutes over medium heat. Now add the salt and peppercorns and mix.

Add the chicken along with the cranberries and mix and cook till you have a dry chicken mix and the chicken is cooked through, which should take around 7 minutes at most. Take off the heat and let cool completely.

Take the smaller pastry round and lightly brush the edges with egg yolk.

Carefully slice off the top and bottom of the Brie, just to make it shorter. Pop the Brie in the center of the round and then add the chicken all around the edge and over the top of the Brie, patting it into a mound and avoiding the brushed egg yolk edge.

Take the second, larger circle and place on top. Push down over the filling, easing out any air bubbles as you go and sealing all around the edges firmly. Brush the top with the egg yolk and pop into the fridge for 30 minutes.

Preheat the oven to 400°F and put a baking sheet in the oven to heat up.

Flute the edge using the back of a knife to create a scalloped edge and score the top. Brush with egg yolk again and bake for 25 to 30 minutes. If the pastry is looking very dark after 20 minutes, cover loosely with foil and lower the oven temperature to 350°F. Serve straight from the oven.

tomato galette

Serves 4 **Prep** 25 minutes
Cook 45 minutes

For the pastry

1 cup/125g all-purpose flour

1 cup/100g chickpea flour

a pinch of salt

7 tablespoons/100g unsalted butter

3–4 tablespoons/ 45–60ml cold water (may need less or more)

For the filling

2 tablespoons vegetable oil

1 clove of garlic, crushed

3 anchovies or ½ teaspoon salt

11 oz/325g cherry tomatoes, halved

1 teaspoon smoked paprika

1 tablespoon tamarind paste

⅔ cup/120g corn kernels (from ½ of a 15¼-oz/430g can, drained)

¼ cup/60g hummus

a small handful of capers

a small handful of fresh basil

This is somewhat like a pizza, but with a few differences. It has a crust, tomatoes, and toppings, but is easier and quicker to make from scratch, while still just as delicious.

Start by making the pastry. Combine the flours and salt in a bowl with the butter and rub the butter in till you have a mix that looks like breadcrumbs.

Add the water 1 tablespoon at a time and mix and squeeze the mixture until it starts to come together. As soon as you have a mound of pastry, bring it together and wrap in plastic wrap, flatten, and chill in the fridge while you cook the tomatoes.

Warm the oil in a pan and, as soon as the oil is hot, add the garlic and anchovies and, using the back of a spoon, push the anchovies and squeeze till they are broken down. This will add seasoning.

Now add the tomatoes along with the paprika and cook on medium heat for 3 to 4 minutes, until they are just starting to soften slightly. Add the tamarind and corn and cook gently for about 10 minutes, till the mixture is fairly dry. Take off the heat.

Preheat the oven to 400°F and pop a baking sheet in the oven to heat up.

Roll the pastry out to about ¼ inch/5mm thick on a piece of parchment paper—this will just make it easier to move onto the sheet later. This does not have to be an even round—being a little rough around the edges will add to the texture.

As soon as you have a rough circle, spoon the hummus in the center and spread all over, leaving about 2 inches/5cm around the edges. Now add all your tomato and corn mixture on top and bring the edges over to create a "crust" as such—you can be as rough as you like. If the pastry breaks up at the edges, just pinch it together. This is quite a brittle dough so you may find it cracks as you fold it over. Pinch it back together and it will be just fine.

Place on the heated sheet, pop into the oven, and bake for 25 to 30 minutes.

As soon as it is out, roughly chop the capers and rip up the basil and sprinkle all over the top. Serve sliced into wedges.

chapter four

DESSERTS

tutti-frutti pavlova

For the meringue

4 large egg whites

1¼ cups/250g granulated sugar

1 teaspoon white vinegar

2 teaspoons cornstarch

1 teaspoon vanilla extract

butter, for lightly greasing the baking sheet

For the tutti-frutti cream

1½ cups/350ml heavy cream

3 tablespoons confectioners' sugar

1 tablespoon cornstarch

½ cup/100g candied (glacé) cherries, chopped

¾ cup/100g pistachios, roughly chopped

1⅓ cups/100g mixed candied peel, chopped if large

For decoration

scant 1 oz/25g dark chocolate shavings

Serves 8   **Prep** 25 minutes   **Cook** 1 hour, plus cooling   **Best eaten** straightaway but will keep in the fridge for 1 day

---

My earliest memory of "tutti-frutti" is of cakes we used to buy at the local Asian supermarket. They came lined up on a tray wrapped in see-through plastic, with all their glorious tutti-frutti on show. They always looked so inviting. Anything with that same delicious color is a winner for me, so I've laced it with a simple whipped cream that sits happily on a chewy meringue nest.

Preheat the oven to 300°F and lightly grease a baking sheet. Using a pencil, trace around a 10-inch/25cm plate onto parchment paper and then flip it over onto the greased baking sheet. Make sure the paper sticks so it doesn't flap in the oven.

For the meringue, put the egg whites in a bowl and whisk until soft peaks start to form, then slowly add the sugar a spoonful at a time, allowing the crystals to melt. As soon as you have used all the sugar and you have stiff peaks, add the vinegar, cornstarch, and vanilla and whisk one last time to incorporate.

Spoon or pipe the meringue into the circle on the parchment paper, as neatly or roughly as you like. Create a slight indent in the center, where your cream will sit.

Bake in the oven for 1 hour. When the hour is up, turn the oven off and leave the meringue in there until the oven is totally cold.

Pop onto a serving dish or store in an airtight container till you are ready to serve.

Put the cream in a bowl with the confectioners' sugar and cornstarch and whisk until you have soft peaks. Add about half of the chopped cherries, pistachios, and mixed peel and gently fold them in, reserving the rest for the top.

I like to take two spoons and dollop the cream mixture onto the meringue in a rough fashion. Finally, scatter the rest of the cherries, pistachios, and mixed peel on top and sprinkle all over with the chocolate shavings.

roasted fruit cobbler

Serves 8 **Prep** 30 minutes **Cook** 35 minutes
Best eaten straightaway but will keep in the fridge for 2 days

For the fruity layer

melted butter, for brushing the dish

4 plums

4 peaches

¼ cup/50g granulated sugar

2 tablespoons cornstarch

¾ cup/125g blueberries

1 lemon

a small handful of fresh mint, chopped

For the cobbles

½ cup + 2 tablespoons/150g unsalted butter, softened

¾ cup/150g granulated sugar

3 large eggs

1¼ cups/150g all-purpose flour

2 teaspoons baking powder

½ cup + 2 teaspoons/50g dried shredded coconut

⅓ cup/30g cocoa powder

⅓ cup/50g chocolate chips, or roughly chopped chocolate

a sprinkling of salt

To serve

ice cream

1¾ oz/50g milk chocolate, melted

The fruit layer at the bottom of this cobbler is the sweet and colorful foundation for my unconventional chocolate coconut cobbles. Delicious to look at, delicious to eat, but satisfyingly simple to make, this dessert is a firm favorite in our house.

Start by getting a medium roasting dish, about 9 x 13 inches/23 x 33cm. Brush the bottom generously with butter. Preheat the oven to 375°F.

Cut the plums into quarters, cut the peaches into eighths, remove the pits, and drop the flesh into a large bowl. Sprinkle with the sugar and cornstarch and mix well until everything is evenly coated. Pour the mixture into the prepared dish and level the top. Sprinkle in the blueberries and finely grate the lemon zest on top, making sure you get it all. Finally, scatter the mint, pushing the leaves in a little so they don't burn when baked.

Now, make the cobbles by putting the butter in a bowl with the sugar and the eggs and mixing by hand or using electric beaters. Add the flour, baking powder, coconut, and cocoa powder and mix well until you have a stiff cake batter. Add the choc chips and mix them in.

Take an ice cream scoop or use two large spoons and dollop the mixture sporadically all over the fruit, leaving little gaps in between.

Sprinkle the cobbles with a little salt and bake in the oven for 35 minutes, until the fruit is soft, the cobbles are crunchy, and you are ready to eat this bad boy!

We like to eat this with ice cream and a drizzling of melted milk chocolate.

→

brigadeiro with sweet and salty pita chips

For the brigadeiro	For the chips
2 x 14-oz/397g cans of condensed milk	6 pita breads, cut into strips
¾ cup/60g cocoa powder	½ cup + 2 tablespoons/ 150g unsalted butter, melted
¼ cup/50g unsalted butter	1 teaspoon sea salt flakes
oil, for greasing the bowl	¼ cup/55g demerara sugar
6 passion fruit	cocoa powder, for dusting (optional)

> **Serves** 6–8   **Prep** 25 minutes, plus chilling
> **Cook** 30 minutes   **Can be assembled** up to 24 hours in advance

This is a sharing dessert, which is not always my favorite way of eating dessert, as I'm usually more of an "all mine" kind of girl, but for this I make an exception. It's a chocolatey set ganache, which sits in a dish, surrounded by homemade pita chips that are baked in butter, salt, and sugar. It's rich and sweet, so I like to drizzle the top with passion fruit pulp to add some freshness.

Start by making the brigadeiro. Put the condensed milk in a nonstick pan along with the cocoa powder and butter and mix everything well.

Have ready a domed bowl, 4¾–6 inches/12–15cm in diameter and large enough to hold all the mixture in the pan. Grease the inside of the bowl and cover the bottom and inside with plastic wrap, making sure to leave some overhanging. Grease inside lightly too.

Pop the condensed milk pan onto high heat. As soon as it comes to a boil, lower the heat and mix constantly for 5 minutes, until it begins to thicken, then take off the heat. Let cool in the pan for 5 minutes before pouring into the prepared bowl. Allow to cool, then chill in the fridge for 4 hours, until it's firm to the touch.

Now, get on to the pita chips. Preheat the oven to 350°F.

Arrange the pita on a large baking sheet lined with parchment paper and drizzle with the melted butter, making sure it coats all the pita chips. Mix the salt and sugar in a bowl and then sprinkle all over the pita chips. Pop into the oven and bake for 20 to 25 minutes, turning them halfway so that they get a fair chance of getting crisp on both sides, then take them out and let cool on the sheet.

When you are ready to serve, pop the bowl of brigadeiro onto a serving dish that's large enough to have the pita chips around the edge. Dust the pita chips with cocoa powder, if you like, and arrange them all around the bowl. Halve the passion fruits, scoop out the pulp, and drizzle all over the brigadeiro.

Take a knife and help yourself to chunks of the brigadeiro, eaten on your crisp salty-sweet pita chips.

earl grey sticky toffee pudding

Serves 10   **Prep** 40 minutes, plus infusing and cooling   **Cook** 45 minutes
Will keep wrapped and in a tin for 3–4 days (and sauce will keep in the fridge for 1 week)

For the cake

¾ cup + 2 tablespoons/ 200ml hot water

4 Earl Grey tea bags

1 star anise

7 oz/200g pitted dates

¼ cup/60g unsalted butter, + extra for greasing the pan

1 cup/200g light or dark muscovado sugar

1 teaspoon baking soda

1 large egg, lightly beaten

½ teaspoon salt

1⅔ cups/200g all-purpose flour, sifted

2½ teaspoons baking powder

For the sauce

1 cup/200g dark muscovado sugar

¼ cup/65g unsalted butter

3 tablespoons molasses

1¼ cups/300ml heavy cream

To serve

ice cream

This is like any yummy sticky toffee pudding, but with a slight difference—all the stickiness of dates and a rich, dark sauce, but enhanced with the subtle scent of Earl Grey tea.

Start by making the cake. Put the hot water in a pitcher or bowl along with the tea bags and star anise and set aside to infuse for 15 minutes.

Meanwhile, preheat the oven to 350°F and grease and line the inside of an 8½ x 4½-inch/900g loaf pan.

Put the pitted dates in a saucepan along with the butter and sugar. Squeeze the tea bags out of the pitcher, making sure to really press out all that flavor. Remove the anise and strain the tea into the pan.

Put on the stove and bring to a boil, then stir and take off as soon as the sugar has dissolved and the butter melted. Let cool for 15 minutes. Using an immersion blender or food processor, blend the mixture to a smooth paste, then transfer to a bowl.

Add the baking soda, egg, salt, flour, and baking powder and mix by hand, with electric beaters, or in a stand mixer until you have a smooth batter. Pour it into the prepared pan and smooth off the edges by tapping on the worktop. Bake for 40 to 50 minutes.

For the sauce, put the sugar, butter, and molasses in a saucepan and place on medium heat until the sugar has dissolved and the butter has melted. As soon as it begins to bubble, take off the heat.

Add the cream and mix in, pop back onto low heat, and allow to bubble away for 5 minutes, until you have a smooth dark caramel.

Take the cake out of the oven and let cool in the pan for 10 minutes. Remove from the pan onto a serving dish and cut into 10 slices, angled just slightly, so they tip a little bit on their sides. Pour the toffee sauce over the top generously, making sure to leave some behind for people who like to pour a little extra, like me! Serve the pudding while it's still warm, with a mahoosive dollop of ice cream alongside.

jam roly-poly

Serves 6   **Prep** 25 minutes
Cook 1 hour

For the roly-poly

2 cups/250g all-purpose flour, + extra for dusting

1 tablespoon baking powder

½ teaspoon salt

¼ cup/50g unsalted butter, cold and cubed, + extra for greasing

1 tablespoon granulated sugar

1 teaspoon vanilla bean paste

¼ cup/50g vegetable shortening

½ cup + 2 tablespoons/ 150ml cold whole milk (you may need less)

For the jam filling

¾ cup/100g fresh raspberries

1 orange, finely grated zest only

1 teaspoon granulated sugar

To finish

¼ cup/ 50g granulated sugar, for dusting

hot custard (see page 118—Tottenham cake)

fresh mixed berries

This is my husband's absolute favorite—he remembers it fondly from his school dinners. Nothing makes me happier than baking this for him. My version is made with fresh fruit (never from frozen—we can't go back to school), a sprinkling of orange zest, and a crunchy sugar topping and is served with custard and berries.

Preheat the oven to 350°F. Place a deep baking pan into the bottom of the oven, add boiling water, and close the oven. Make sure there is a rack above the pan, as this is where the jam roly-poly will steam.

Take a 12 x 16-inch/30 x 40cm sheet of foil and a piece of parchment paper that is the same size and pop the paper on top of the foil. Grease the paper and set both aside.

Pour the flour into a bowl along with the baking powder, salt, butter, sugar, and vanilla bean paste. Rub the butter in, using the tips of your fingers, until you have no more massive clumps of butter and the mixture resembles breadcrumbs. You could equally do this using a food processor.

Add the shortening and mix in well. Make a well in the center and add ½ cup/120ml of the milk to it. Using a rubber spatula, bring the dough together, then get your hands in to bring it into a ball. If the dough is looking dry, add the remaining milk.

Dust the surface with some flour, pop the dough down, and roll into a 10-inch/25cm square.

Crush the raspberries with the orange zest and mix well with the sugar. Spread the fruit onto the dough square, leaving a ½-inch/1cm edge exposed.

Now roll like you would a cinnamon bun, making sure the seam is on the bottom. Pinch the ends to seal it really well. Pick it up and put into the center of the paper, seam-side down. Bring the two paper edges to the top and roll to seal, making sure to leave lots of space for the roly-poly to grow. Seal the ends by rolling them up, then put the roly-poly on the rack and steam and bake for 1 hour.

As soon as it is baked, take out and let cool for 10 minutes in the paper foil parcel. Unwrap, pop onto a serving dish, and sprinkle sugar over the top generously. Cut into slices while still warm and serve with hot custard and fresh berries.

filo cream parcels

For the cream

5 cups/1.2 liters heavy cream

1 cup/120g ground rice or rice flour

½ cup/100g granulated sugar

1 orange, finely grated zest only (save the juice for the syrup)

For the filo casing

9½-oz/270g package of filo pastry

7 tablespoons/100g ghee or butter, melted

For the syrup

1 cup/200g granulated sugar

juice of 1 orange, adding extra water to make up to ¾ cup + 2 tablespoons/200ml

1 teaspoon orange blossom water

3 cardamom pods, seeds removed and crushed

pinch of saffron strands

⅓ cup/50g pistachios, finely chopped

Makes 14   **Prep** 30 minutes, plus cooling and soaking   **Cook** 40 minutes
Best eaten on the day they are made but will keep in the fridge for up to 24 hours

---

This is my version of a Lebanese dessert. Filo pastry is filled with a reduced cream thickened with ground rice and then sweetened and flavored with zingy orange zest. I bake these until they are super crisp to balance out that soft filling.

Warm the cream in a fairly deep saucepan on high heat. As soon as it comes to a boil, turn down to medium heat and keep stirring for about 10 minutes, until it has reduced and thickened to make it richer.

Lower the heat, pour in your ground rice, and whisk for 2 to 3 minutes, until it really begins to thicken up. As soon as it starts to thicken and come away from the sides, take off the heat, add the sugar and orange zest, and mix well. Pour onto a flat plate, smooth out, and let cool as much as possible.

Preheat the oven to 400°F.

Cut the pile of rectangular filo sheets down the middle into 14 squares. Lay them out and dollop an equal amount of the cooled cream mixture into the center

of each (if you want to be exact, it's about 3 oz/85g each). Take a square, fold one side over, then the next, and then the next, working your way round until you have encased the mound into a neat square, roughly 2¾ inches/7cm. Repeat with the remaining squares.

Generously brush two baking sheets with the ghee, add the squares seam-side down, and brush the tops with more ghee. Pop into the oven for 15 to 20 minutes to really crisp up the pastry.

Meanwhile, make the syrup by mixing the sugar, orange juice and water, orange blossom water, cardamom, and saffron in a small pot. Give it a stir and, as soon as it comes to a boil, decrease the heat to low and cook for 10 minutes to thicken slightly.

As soon as the pastries are cooked and golden, pop them onto a serving dish and pour the syrup all over to soak into the filo. Allow to soak for 30 minutes.

These can be eaten as they are or are also delicious served chilled, which lets them firm up a little. Sprinkle with a tiny bit of pistachio just before serving.

sharing molten chocolate cake

Serves 4–5	**Prep** 15 minutes
Cook 22 minutes	

7 tablespoons/100g unsalted butter, softened, + extra melted for greasing the dish

2 tablespoons cocoa powder

3½ oz/100g dark chocolate, chopped

2 large eggs

2 large egg yolks

½ cup + 2 tablespoons/120g granulated sugar

¾ cup/100g all-purpose flour, sifted

a pinch of salt

To finish

confectioners' sugar for dusting

crème fraîche to serve

If you don't mind sharing, this is the one for you. It's like those little melt-in-the-middle chocolate cakes, but a large one. With none of the individual pots, there's less washing up and still all of the deliciousness. But I do often find myself asking, because it is just one pot, does that mean it is technically one portion? Can it all be mine, mine, mine? This is best served hot and enjoyed with a dollop of cooling crème fraîche.

Preheat the oven to 350°F. Start by greasing a 9-inch/23cm nonstick or enamel pie dish (I use an 8½ x 1¾ inches/22 x 4.5cm deep enamel pie dish). Using a pastry brush, brush melted butter on the bottom and right up the sides of the dish in the same direction until you have covered it all with butter.

Pop into the freezer for 5 minutes. Take out of the freezer, sprinkle with the cocoa powder, and tip the dish around so that the butter catches the cocoa. Do this until you have totally covered the dish, then tap out any excess cocoa powder. Put the dish into the fridge while you make the batter.

Now, to make the cake, put the butter into a glass dish along with the chocolate and melt either over a pot of simmering water or in the microwave in 30-second bursts on low, stirring in between. Once the butter and chocolate are totally melted and mixed, let cool.

In another bowl, combine the whole eggs, egg yolks, and sugar and whisk till the mixture is light and fluffy. This should take 2 to 3 minutes using electric beaters on high. Add the melted chocolate and butter mix and whisk in till you have an even mixture. Fold the flour and salt into the wet mixture till there are no more bits of flour.

Take the dish out of the fridge, pour the mixture into the dish, and allow it to run and level off naturally. Bake for 17 to 18 minutes. The cake should be set around the sides and on top, but still gooey in the middle. As soon as the timer is up, put a plate on top and turn the cake out.

To serve, dust with confectioners' sugar, add a dollop of the crème fraîche, and dig in while it is still hot. This needs to be eaten straightaway, as it carries on cooking if left and the gooey middle will start to set—and we don't want that to happen!

slow-cooker apple and tarragon crumble

For the apple base

6 green apples (you want a tart apple, something with a tang), peeled, cored, and cut into thin wedges, about 1 pound 2 oz/500g in weight

¼ cup/50g unsalted butter, melted

2 tablespoons/25g granulated sugar

small handful of fresh tarragon, leaves picked and finely chopped

1 cup/150g fresh or frozen blackberries

a pinch of salt

1 x 14-oz/397g can of caramel

For the cakey top

2 cups/250g all-purpose flour

1 tablespoon baking powder

½ teaspoon salt

1 cup + 2 tablespoons/ 250g unsalted butter, softened

1¼ cups/250g granulated sugar

1 teaspoon vanilla extract

1 teaspoon almond extract

To serve

hot custard (see page 118—Tottenham cake) and/or ice cream

Serves 6   **Prep** 25 minutes
Cook 5–6 hours in a slow cooker

This is the kind of dessert I like to make when my oven is full of everything else and there is no room for dessert—and on no planet is that acceptable. There is always room for dessert, in our hearts, in our kitchens, on our plates! So this is the perfect recipe for such a situation: stewed apples, brought to life with fresh tarragon, topped with a crumb layer that miraculously turns itself into a cakey top that's just insanely delicious!

Begin by putting the apple wedges in a slow cooker dish. Add the melted butter and sugar and mix well. Now add the chopped tarragon and blackberries and mix them in with the pinch of salt.

Level off the apple layer, then spoon in the can of caramel and create an even layer on top of the apple by spreading it to the edges with the back of a spoon.

To make the cakey top, combine the flour, baking powder, salt, and butter in another bowl and rub together until you have a breadcrumby mixture. Add the sugar, vanilla, and almond extract and mix until smooth and even—you can do this by hand or in a food processor, whichever you prefer. Spoon the whole lot onto the caramel layer in an even-ish layer.

Pop the dish into the slow cooker, turn onto the lowest setting, put the lid on, and cook for 5 to 6 hours.

Once it's ready, you should be able to spoon the delicious appley, caramelly crumble straight out of the pan. We like to eat this with hot custard and a dollop of ice cream. It's all or nothing here!

chocolate caramel flan

Serves 10–12
Prep 40 minutes
Cook 1 hour, plus cooling
Keeps in the fridge for 2 days

For the bottom

⅓ cup + 1 tablespoon/125g salted caramel sauce

For the cake

½ cup + 2 tablespoons/150g unsalted butter, softened, + extra melted butter for greasing the pan

¾ cup + 2 tablespoons/190g brown sugar

1 large egg

1 tablespoon vanilla extract

1⅔ cups/200g all-purpose flour, sifted, + extra for flouring the tin

⅓ cup/30g cocoa powder

1 teaspoon baking soda

1 teaspoon baking powder

3 tablespoons instant coffee

1 cup/240ml whole milk

For the crème caramel

2½ cups/600ml evaporated milk

1 x 14-oz/397g can of condensed milk

4 large eggs

1 teaspoon vanilla bean paste

a pinch of salt

This clever dessert starts with caramel in the pan, then adds a simple chocolate cake batter and finally a crème caramel mixture, and as it sits and bakes in a water bath, the crème caramel seeps down to meet the caramel and creates a beautiful soft layer, which becomes the top once the cake is turned out. Just magical!

Preheat the oven to 350°F. Grease and lightly flour the inside of a 9-inch/23cm bundt pan. Find a roasting dish big enough to hold the bundt pan comfortably and deep enough for water to come two-thirds of the way up the side of the bundt pan. Pop a tea towel into the bottom of the roasting dish.

Put the salted caramel in a microwaveable dish and warm for just long enough to make it runny, about 20 seconds. Pour into the pan, avoiding drips on the sides. Tap on the worktop to level the surface.

Make the cake by beating the butter and sugar in a mixing bowl until you have a really light and fluffy mixture. Add the egg and vanilla extract and mix in. In a separate bowl, combine the flour, cocoa, baking soda, and baking powder and mix really well.

Now, spoon the coffee into a small bowl, add a few tablespoons of the milk and heat for a few seconds in the microwave, until the coffee has dissolved. Mix, pour into the remaining milk, and stir well.

Sift a third of the flour mixture onto the butter, sugar, and egg mixture and fold in with a large metal spoon. Fold in a third of the milk mixture, then repeat until all the flour and milk has been mixed in.

When you have a smooth batter, spoon it over the salted caramel, tap the pan on the worktop to remove any bubbles, and make sure you have a level top. Put the bundt pan into the center of the roasting dish.

Make the crème caramel mixture by mixing the evaporated milk, condensed milk, eggs, vanilla, and salt in a food processor until smooth and even. Pour on top of the cake batter and level the top.

Have a kettle of hot water ready. Put the roasting dish with the bundt pan into the oven. Before you close the door, pour the water straight onto the tea towel in the roasting dish, making sure the water reaches at least two-thirds of the way up. Bake for 1 hour and don't be tempted to open the oven. Once cooked, take out and let cool in the pan for another hour, then flip over onto a serving dish and it is ready to eat.

croissant ice cream pudding

butter, at room temperature, for greasing the dish and spreading

4 large croissants

½ cup/170g marmalade, fine shred or smooth, whatever you prefer

12¼ oz/350g vanilla ice cream, softened

2 oz/60g dark chocolate, chopped

confectioners' sugar, for dusting

Serves 6 **Prep** 10 minutes, plus 10 minutes standing **Cook** 10–12 minutes

This is based on a bread-and-butter pudding, but made with croissants because they are much more buttery, then smothered with extra butter and copious amounts of thick marmalade. It's also much faster than a regular bread-and-butter pudding because I'm making it with ice cream—not just popping some on the side or on top, but actually making the pudding with it! Traditionally made with custard and milk, it seemed like the perfect shortcut. Sprinkle with some dark chocolate and this might be the fastest and most buttery pudding you will make, ever.

Preheat the oven to 400°F. Start by greasing a medium rectangular roasting dish with some butter; be generous!

Slice the croissants lengthwise, all the way. Butter the inside of all eight slices with a thin layer of butter, then take the marmalade and spread with a layer of that.

Place the croissants into the dish, arranging them in some sort of neat fashion. Take dollops of the ice cream, dot around sporadically, and allow to just melt a little for 10 minutes. It won't melt completely; the structure will still be quite fluffy on top.

Sprinkle the chocolate over the top. Pop into the oven and bake for 10 to 12 minutes. Dust with some confectioners' sugar and it is ready to eat.

chai chia puddings

Serves 4   **Prep** 15 minutes, plus soaking

⅓ cup/60g chia seeds

1⅔ cups/400ml hazelnut milk

3 tablespoons masala chai mix (see page 164)

2 tablespoons maple syrup, + extra for drizzling

1 mango, diced, about 2 cups (11½ oz/325g)

1 cup/200g mango pulp (if you can't find any, you can make this by just whizzing up some chopped mango)

⅔ cup/200g Greek yogurt

¼ cup/40g roasted chopped hazelnuts

Chia seeds are not just for breakfast, they are for pudding too. When you soak them in nut milk they make a thick, creamy pudding, my version of which is fragrantly delicious with chai spices, served with chopped mango, and topped with yogurt, maple syrup, and roasted hazelnuts. I think I just like saying chai chia. Go on, say it. It rolls off the tongue!

This is super simple. Pop the chia seeds into a bowl along with the hazelnut milk and mix really well. Sprinkle in the chai spices and the maple syrup and mix again well.

Cover with some plastic wrap and chill for at least 4 hours to allow the chia seeds to bloom (there's nothing worse than crunchy, unbloomed chia seeds). Alternatively, use a plastic container with a lid rather than a bowl and plastic wrap.

The next stage is to add the chopped mango and stir. This is perfect to chill overnight if you are doing it for breakfast, but do this at breakfast time if you are making the puddings for lunch or dinner.

Take four empty jam jars or glass serving dishes. Equally divide the mango pulp among the jars, then the chia pudding. Add the yogurt and drizzle with some maple syrup. Sprinkle the hazelnuts over the top and these are ready to serve.

tottenham cake
with custard

Makes 24 small squares and 1 quart/1 liter of custard   **Prep** 35 minutes   **Cook** 45 minutes, plus cooling   **Will keep** in a tin for up to 3 days (and custard will keep in fridge for up to 3 days)

First invented in 1901, in Tottenham no less, this cake is topped with a pink icing that was originally colored using mulberries. I would like to say that my first experience of this steeped-in-history baked treat was driven by my need for baking knowledge, but sadly it was not. This was the cake I remembered from school lunchtimes: simple, delicious, and sweet, all doused in hot custard. I had forgotten about it until I recently stopped off at a main-street bakery and there it was again, though with less appeal when there is no queue to wait in or teenagers to fend off. My purchase didn't match up to my memories, so I decided to try making it for myself, and here's the outcome. Don't get me wrong, though; on a busy day I would very happily devour the bakery-bought variety.

For the cake

1¼ cups/280g unsalted butter, softened, + extra for greasing the pan

1¼ cups + 2 tablespoons/ 280g granulated sugar

5 large eggs

1¼ teaspoons vanilla extract

1¼ teaspoons almond extract

2 cups + 6 tablespoons/ 300g all-purpose flour, sifted

4½ teaspoons baking powder

½ teaspoon salt

5 tablespoons/75 ml whole milk

For the icing

1 cup/125g fresh raspberries

3½ cups/440g confectioners' sugar, sifted

For the custard

1 cup/240ml heavy cream

3⅔ cups/875ml whole milk

5 large egg yolks

3 tablespoons + 2 teaspoons cornstarch

½ cup + 2 tablespoons/ 125g granulated sugar

1¼ teaspoons vanilla extract

2½ teaspoons almond extract

Start by making the cake. Preheat the oven to 350°F and line and grease a 9 x 13-inch/23 x 33cm baking pan.

Put the butter in a bowl with the sugar and beat until the mixture is light and fluffy and almost white. Now add the eggs, one at a time, until incorporated. Add the vanilla, almond extract, flour, baking powder, salt, and milk and fold them in until all the flour has disappeared. Pour into the prepared pan and level the surface, then bake for 30 to 35 minutes, until a skewer inserted comes out clean. Take out and let cool completely in the pan.

Make the icing by crushing the raspberries using the back of a fork until you have no lumps, apart from the seeds of course. Add the confectioners' sugar and mix until you have a beautiful pink icing, with not just color, but also that fresh raspberry flavor.

Tip the cake out onto a serving dish and then smother all over with the pink icing.

Let's get on to that custard by combining the cream and milk in a pan, gently bringing the mixture to a boil, and then turning the heat off.

Combine the egg yolks, cornstarch, sugar, vanilla, and almond extract in a bowl and whisk to a smooth paste. Now, in a gentle stream, add the hot milk mixture, a little at a time, whisking all the time. Once all the milk has been added, pour back into the pan, pop back onto low to medium heat, and stir until the custard coats the back of the spoon. Take off the heat and transfer to a small pitcher.

Now you are ready to eat your soft cake, with its sweet icing, all doused in hot custard. Just like in high school.

chapter five

CELEBRATION BAKES

mango and coconut yogurt cake
with german buttercream

For the cake

butter, for greasing the pans

½ cup/50g dried shredded coconut

1 mango, peeled and thinly sliced lengthwise

1⅓ cups + 1 tablespoon/ 400g Greek yogurt

1½ cups/300g granulated sugar

7 large eggs, lightly beaten

3¼ cups/400g all-purpose flour

5¾ teaspoons baking powder

¾ teaspoon salt

For the German buttercream

½ cup + 2 tablespoons/ 150ml whole milk

½ cup/100g granulated sugar

3 large egg yolks

1 tablespoon cornstarch

1½ cups/350g unsalted butter, at room temperature

½ teaspoon vanilla extract

For the decoration

¾ cup/150g mango pulp

¼ cup/25g coconut flakes or dried shredded coconut, toasted

To serve

Greek yogurt and extra mango pulp

Serves 8–10   **Prep** 35 minutes, plus chilling
Cook 45 minutes

These flavors are as traditional as they get for me. They're the flavors I grew up with, though while mango was cooked in curries, dried, or eaten in the sun under the shade of the tree, it was never put in a cake! The same went for coconut. If it wasn't being eaten dry, it was being stewed or eaten early, drinking its sweet water and scooping out its young flesh, but never ever in a cake. So, let's fix that, and put all that wonderful stuff straight into a cake, shall we?

Preheat the oven to 350°F. Line the bottoms and grease two 8-inch/20cm round cake pans.

Toast the coconut in a small pan until it is golden, and sprinkle into the bottoms of the cake pans, making sure to evenly distribute it. Toasting it will enhance the flavor (untoasted coconut is no different to the wood chip shavings I lay out for my rabbit). Add the mango in some sort of orderly fashion, straight on top of that coconut.

The cake is an all-in-one method, so really easy. Pop the yogurt into a large mixing bowl along with the sugar, eggs, flour, baking powder, and salt and

→

mix until you have a smooth, shiny cake batter. Pour the mixture into the pans and tap the pans a few times on the work surface to level off the top. Bake for 40 to 45 minutes, until golden and a skewer inserted comes out clean. Take the cakes out and let cool in the tins for 15 minutes, then turn out and allow to cool completely.

Meanwhile, make the buttercream by putting the milk in a saucepan with the sugar. As soon as it just comes to a boil, take off the heat and mix, making sure the sugar has melted.

Now put the egg yolks in a bowl with the cornstarch and whisk. In a steady stream pour in the hot milk mixture, making sure to stir all of the time. Pour the mixture back into the pan and heat gently until it all thickens into a really thick custard that coats the back of the spoon. Transfer to a large bowl, cover with plastic wrap, and let cool, then chill in the fridge.

When chilled, beat the custard mix, then add a good tablespoon of butter at a time, beating after each addition. Add the vanilla. Keep beating until you have a really stiff, pipeable buttercream. Pop into a piping bag.

Take the first cake, with the fruit side facing upward, and arrange on a serving dish. Pipe swirls of the buttercream all around the edge and then in the center, covering the top of the cake. Pop the other cake on top and make the same swirls around the edge, avoiding the middle and leaving gaps between the swirls.

Pour the mango pulp into the center, allowing it to drip down the sides. Sprinkle it with the toasted coconut and serve the cake with Greek yogurt and any extra mango pulp.

honey cake with salted hazelnuts

Serves 10   Prep 1 hour, plus chilling
Cook 26–28 minutes (baking in four batches of two cookie rounds)

For the cake

6 tablespoons/80g
unsalted butter

¾ cup + 1 tablespoon/
270g honey

½ cup + 2 tablespoons/
120g granulated sugar

2 large eggs, lightly beaten

1 teaspoon baking soda

4 cups/500g all-purpose
flour, sifted, + extra for
dusting

For the filling

2½ cups/570ml sour cream

⅔ cup/80g confectioners'
sugar

1 cup/240ml heavy cream

3 tablespoons honey

1 teaspoon vanilla bean
paste

For the decoration

⅔ cup/100g roasted
chopped hazelnuts

½ teaspoon salt

fresh berries

This looks like a cake, but in fact it's made with eight cookie-like rounds that are flavored with honey and browned butter, then moistened with a sweet and slightly sour cream and stacked up. The end result is round and cuts like a cake, so that's what I'm calling it, but to be honest I don't care about labels, all I know is it's delicious.

Put the butter in a small saucepan, bring to a boil, then lower the heat and let it begin to brown. As soon as the little grains of milk solids become dark, take off the heat. Add the honey and sugar and heat until the sugar has dissolved, then tip into a large bowl and let cool for 15 minutes.

Add the eggs and mix well. Now add the baking soda and the flour and mix till a smooth dough forms. Cover and chill in the fridge for at least 2 hours.

Roll the dough into a sausage shape and divide into eight equal pieces. You can weigh them if you want to be exact. Dust the work surface and your hands generously and shape the eight pieces into balls.

Line two baking sheets with parchment paper and preheat the oven to 350°F. Find a 7-inch/18cm round template (e.g., a plate or the bottom of a cake pan).

Dust a ball of dough with flour, then place between two sheets of parchment paper and roll out to about ⅓ inch/3mm thick. Use the template to cut it into a circle, being sure to keep all of the scraps. Repeat with all eight balls.

Pop the circles onto the baking sheets (however many will fit) and bake for just 5 to 7 minutes. As soon as they are baked, take off the sheet, pop onto a wire rack, and repeat until you have done all eight.

Arrange the scraps in an even layer across the two sheets and bake for 6 to 8 minutes, until they are really crisp and golden. Take them out and set aside.

Make the filling by mixing together the sour cream and the confectioners' sugar really well. Pour the heavy cream into a bowl and whip to soft peaks. Fold in the sour cream mixture, honey, and vanilla.

It is best to assemble this cake directly onto your serving plate (one that can fit in your fridge). Use a dab of the cream to secure the first circle onto the serving dish. Drop about 5 tablespoons of the cream mixture on top and carefully spread evenly all over. Put the next circle on and repeat until you have done all eight layers.

You should have enough cream to cover the top and sides, so do exactly that and smooth over as best you can. It doesn't have to be perfect, because we are going to really cover this up.

Put the baked scraps in a food processor and blitz to a fine crumb. Mix in the roasted hazelnuts and salt.

For extra decoration I like to use a template to create a heart shape in the crumbs on the top of the cake, but choose whatever shape you like—even use a doily, if you can find one or know what one is! If you don't want to use a template, just mark a heart (or other shape) on the frosting with a butter knife and use that as a guide for where to stick the crumbs.

Take the crumbs and gently press them onto the sides and the top around your template, if using, before removing it. You might have to pipe more frosting onto your shape to neaten up the edges. Now put into the fridge to set and chill.

Serve with some fresh berries.

berry hot cross buns

For the dough

1¼ cups/300ml whole milk

¼ cup/50g unsalted butter

4 cups/500g bread flour, + extra for dusting

6 tablespoons/75g granulated sugar

1 teaspoon salt

1 package (2¼ teaspoons/7g) fast-acting dried yeast

1 large egg, lightly beaten

oil, for greasing the bowl

⅔ cup/75g dried cranberries, roughly chopped

⅓ cup/50g dried blueberries, roughly chopped

1 orange, finely grated zest only

For the berry cross

⅓ oz/9g freeze-dried strawberries or raspberries

⅔ cup/75g all-purpose flour, sifted

6 tablespoons/90ml water

For the filling and glaze

10½-oz/300g jar of seedless berry jam (strawberry, raspberry, whatever you fancy)

3 tablespoons golden syrup or light corn syrup

Makes 15   **Prep** 40 minutes, plus rising   **Cook** 20 minutes
Best eaten on day they are made

I have to admit that hot cross buns were one of my least favorite things growing up. Not that my parents bought them often, but at Easter time we'd have them at school and I never liked the flavor. It's still not my favorite, but the less my body needs butter, the more I crave it. These are a step up from regular hot cross buns, the dough crammed with all the fruitiness of berries, and there's no reason to cut and toast them because they are already filled to the seam with jam. The finishing touch is a pink cross to match!

Start by making the dough. Put the milk in a saucepan with the butter, heat until the butter has melted, and take off the heat.

Put the flour in a large bowl and mix in the sugar. Add the salt on one side of the flour and the yeast to the other side.

→

Make a well in the center, drop in the egg, and then add the warm milk mixture and roughly mix using the back of a spoon or a rubber spatula, then get your hands in and bring the dough together.

On a lightly floured surface, knead the dough until it is smooth and stretchy. This will take about 10 minutes and lots of elbow grease. Or you can do it in a stand mixer with a dough hook attached, which should take about 6 minutes on medium speed. Pop the dough into a greased bowl and let rise in a warm place until doubled in size.

Line a large baking sheet or two smaller sheets with some parchment paper. Tip the dough out onto a lightly floured surface and knock all of that air out. Spread the dough out into a circle and sprinkle with the cranberries, blueberries, and orange zest, then knead the lot in until the fruit is evenly distributed.

Take the dough and divide into 15 portions. Roll each dough ball until it has a smooth surface and pop onto the sheet or sheets with about a 1¼-inch/3cm gap between each one to give them space to rise and grow. Place in a warm spot, covered in some greased plastic wrap, to double in size.

Preheat the oven to 400°F.

Now to make the flour paste for the cross. Pound the strawberries or raspberries in a mortar and pestle or blitz in a food processor until you have a fine pink dust. Put this in a bowl with the flour and water and mix to a smooth, pipeable paste. Spoon into a piping bag. Uncover the risen dough and pipe a thin cross on each bun.

Bake the buns for 18 to 20 minutes. As soon as they are golden brown and bounce back when touched, take them out of the oven and let cool on a cooling rack. Then use the handle of a small spoon or the end of a butter knife to make a hole in the side of each bun without going all the way through. You are creating a cavity to fill with delicious jam.

Pop the jam into a piping bag and pipe it into the hole of each hot cross bun, until full. You will know when it is as the piping bag will naturally force itself out. Put the buns back onto the baking sheet. Warm the golden syrup just to make it runny and brush all over the buns to give them that sweet, sticky glaze. Filled, fruity, and ready to eat!

zesty fruitcake

Serves 12–14
Prep 50 minutes
Cook 1¾ hours

For the cake

1 cup/225g unsalted butter, softened, + extra for greasing the pan

1 grapefruit, ½ the juice and finely grated zest

1 orange, juice and finely grated zest

1 lemon, juice and finely grated zest

1 lime, juice and finely grated zest

9 oz/250g dates, pitted and chopped

1⅓ cups/100g mixed candied peel, chopped if large

½ cup/100g candied (glacé) cherries, chopped

2¾ cups/400g currants

1 large very ripe banana, mashed

4 large eggs

2 tablespoons whole milk

2 cups + 6 tablespoons/ 300g all-purpose flour, sifted

2 teaspoons pumpkin pie spice

1 teaspoon baking powder

For the decoration

¼ cup/80g apricot jam

1 pound 2 oz/500g yellow marzipan

confectioners' sugar, for dusting

1 pound 2 oz/500g white fondant

Fruitcake takes me back to being in high school, where they made a tame version with just a smattering of fruit for our South Asian palates, which perhaps they thought couldn't cope with all the flavors of the "West." It was delicious, but I couldn't understand why there was not as much fruit in it as the ones I remembered seeing on the telly. I love fruitcake just as it is, slabs cut out, with cheese, or custard. This is my very zesty version, sharp from all the citrus, sweet from the dried fruit and dates, but free from refined sugar. It simply doesn't need it. It's delicious enough as it is. But you can, if you want, add a layer of marzipan and fondant, especially if it's for a special occasion or Christmas. Or even if it's just for you—because fruitcake is not just for Christmas and weddings!

Preheat the oven to 325°F. Grease and line the bottom and sides of a 9-inch/23cm round springform pan with parchment paper. Grease again and line a second time, making sure to trim off any excess paper at the top so the paper is in line flush with the top of the pan.

Put the zest of the grapefruit, orange, lemon, and lime into a large bowl. Squeeze all the citrus fruit juice into a liquid measuring cup. We need ¾ cup plus 2 tablespoons/200ml of liquid, so if the juice squeezed doesn't come up to ¾ cup plus 2 tablespoons/200ml, top up with orange juice.

Now add the dates, mixed peel, cherries, and currants to the bowl with the zest. Add the juice and mix well, then allow the fruit to absorb all the moisture. Add the mashed banana and mix.

In a separate bowl, beat the eggs and butter until well combined. Add the milk, flour, pumpkin pie spice, and baking powder and mix to an evenly distributed batter. It might look a little curdled, but this doesn't matter; it bakes just fine.

Add the fruit mixture and mix it in until all the fruit is covered in the batter. Spoon the mixture into the prepared pan and level off the top. Take a large piece of foil, cover the top, and secure the foil around the edge. Bake on the middle shelf for 1 hour.

After 1 hour, take the cake out, remove the foil, and bake for 30 to 45 minutes, until golden and firm on top and a skewer inserted in the middle comes out with no raw batter attached. Take the cake out of the oven, place onto a cooling rack, and let cool in the pan for 30 minutes, before turning out onto the cooling rack and allowing to cool completely.

If you are decorating the cake, once it has cooled completely, melt the jam in a small pan until it is liquid enough to brush on. Brush the surface.

Roll out the marzipan on a surface lightly dusted with confectioners' sugar to a ¼-inch/5mm thickness and large enough to cover the top. Use the cake pan as a template to cut a perfect circle. Take the marzipan circle and place on top of the cake onto the apricot jam and smooth over using the palm of your hand.

Brush again with the leftover jam. Roll the fondant out in the same way as the marzipan and cut a circle out. Pop on top of the marzipan and press gently so it adheres to the marzipan layer.

Use any leftover marzipan and fondant to decorate the top. I quite like to keep it simple and to just use the back of a knife to scallop the edges.

pull-apart muffin cake

For the Swiss meringue buttercream

7 large egg whites

1¾ cups/345g granulated sugar

2⅔ cups/600g unsalted butter, softened

For the chocolate salted caramel

¾ cup + 1 tablespoon/ 175g brown sugar

¼ cup/50g unsalted butter, softened

½ teaspoon salt

½ cup + 2 tablespoons/ 150ml heavy cream

7 oz/200g dark chocolate, chopped or chips

For the cupcakes

1 cup + 2 tablespoons/ 250g unsalted butter, softened

1¼ cups/250g granulated sugar

4 large eggs

½ teaspoon salt

2 cups/250g all-purpose flour, sifted

1 tablespoon baking powder

⅓ cup/30g cocoa powder

5 tablespoons/75ml whole milk

For the decoration

15 marshmallows (regular size)

candied (glacé) cherries

rainbow sprinkles

Makes 24 cakes **Prep** 1½ hours
Cook 40 minutes

This cake can be as large or as small as you want. What I love about it is that there is no cutting or slicing or plating involved, as it's made from cupcakes, which are filled with a chocolate salted caramel, then wedged together and frosted with a delicious Swiss meringue buttercream, all to look like one single cake!

Begin by making the Swiss meringue buttercream. Put the egg whites and sugar in a large bowl and mix together. It will feel stiff, but try to incorporate them.

Find a pot that the bowl will sit on comfortably. Pour about 1½ inches/4cm of water into the pot and bring to a boil, then lower the heat to medium and pop a tea towel on top, so it is just covering the pot but not touching the water. This is going to act like a hammock for the bowl, so place your bowl straight on top and mix constantly for 15 to 20 minutes. The aim is for the mixture to get to about 161°F/72°C and the sugar to dissolve—you will need a thermometer for this.

As soon as it reaches the right temperature, take off the heat and transfer the mixture to the bowl of a stand mixer. Whisk on high for 10 to 15 minutes, until the bowl becomes cool to the touch and the meringue is stiff.

→

Now take off the whisk attachment and replace it with the paddle attachment. Pinch off 2-inch/5cm pieces of butter and drop them into the mixture, waiting for each one to be incorporated before adding the next. Continue until you have used up all the butter. The mixture will appear liquid, but keep mixing for another 5 to 10 minutes and it will thicken. As soon as it's no longer runny and you can spoon it up, it is ready. If you find the mixture is still runny, pop the bowl in the fridge for 2 hours, then start mixing it again. It should really thicken up enough to be able to pipe beautifully. Set the buttercream aside or pop it in the fridge if you are using it later.

Make the caramel by combining the brown sugar and butter in a pot and heating until the sugar dissolves.

As soon as it begins to boil, take off the heat, mix in the salt and cream, then pop it back onto the stove and heat for another 3 minutes, until it begins to bubble and thicken. Have the chocolate ready in a bowl. Pour the hot caramel all over it and mix until the chocolate has melted. Let cool.

To make the cupcakes, line two 12-hole muffin pans with cupcake liners. Preheat the oven to 375°F and make sure you have two oven shelves free.

Combine the butter and sugar in a mixing bowl and beat until the mixture is light and fluffy. Add the eggs one at a time with the salt, and then add the flour, baking powder, and cocoa powder and fold them in until you have a smooth batter. Finally, fold in the milk to loosen the batter a little.

Dollop into the cupcake liners and tap the pans sharply on the work surface to level the tops. Bake for about 15 minutes. Take out of the oven and let cool in the pans for 10 minutes, then lift out of the pans and let cool on a wire rack. As soon as the muffins are totally cool, which won't take long, use an apple corer to remove the center of each cake, making sure not to go all the way to the bottom.

Pop the caramel into a piping bag and fill each cavity. Using the little rounded tops of the cakes you just pulled out, cover the cavities—the rest of the cores you can nibble on.

Now get yourself a big rectangular serving board. Remove the cupcakes from their paper liners and place them in a rectangle shape, four cupcakes by six, to make 24. Once you know exactly where they are going, get some of that meringue buttercream and dollop a little on the bottom of each cake to just secure them in place and prevent them from moving around.

Fill each diamond-shaped gap between the muffins with a marshmallow. Now we are ready to frost. Dollop equal amounts of buttercream on top of each muffin and, using a spatula, spread as if you were frosting just one cake, frost the sides then neaten up the edges and level off the top. It should look like one large rectangular cake. Pop the remaining buttercream into a piping bag and pipe kisses all around the edge. Pop a little cherry on top of each, a scattering of rainbow sprinkles, and all it needs are candles and 24 people!

cola cake

Serves 9–12
Prep 40 minutes
Cook 55 minutes
Keeps in the fridge
for 2 days

For the cake

unsalted butter

1¾ cups/225g all-
purpose flour, sifted

1 cup + 2 tablespoons/
225g granulated
sugar

1 cup/85g cocoa
powder, sifted

1½ teaspoons baking
powder

1½ teaspoons baking
soda

2 teaspoons instant
coffee

1 cup/240ml whole milk

2 large eggs

½ cup/120ml
vegetable oil

1 cup/240ml cola,
reserving the extra
⅓ cup/80ml

For the caramel

1⅓ cups/330ml cola, +
the extra ⅓ cup/80ml

1 tablespoon dark brown
sugar

juice of ½ lime
(1 tablespoon)

2 tablespoons unsalted
butter

½ cup + 2 tablespoons/
150ml heavy cream

pinch ground cinnamon

For the buttercream

½ cup/100g vegetable
shortening, at room
temperature

3½ oz/100g full-fat
cream cheese

3¼ cups/400g
confectioners' sugar,
sifted

1 teaspoon vanilla extract

I'm not a massive fan of cola as a drink, because although I quite like the flavor, my body just doesn't appreciate the carbonated element. There's nothing worse than needing to burp when I'm midway through a meeting, or talking to other parents at the school gate, or just trying to do life. So I have found a different use for cola and added it to a cake instead!

Preheat the oven to 350°F. Line and grease a 9-inch/23cm square cake pan.

Combine the flour, sugar, cocoa powder, baking powder, baking soda, and instant coffee in a large bowl and mix until fully combined.

Combine the milk, eggs, and oil in a pitcher or bowl and whisk well. Pour into the dry mixture and mix. Now add your cola, whisk until you have a very liquid batter, and pour into the prepared pan. Bake on the middle shelf for 55 minutes.

Meanwhile, make the caramel by pouring the cola into a small saucepan and bringing to a boil. Lower the heat slightly and allow it to boil for 18 to 20 minutes, until syrupy and really reduced.

Take the pan off the heat and add the brown sugar, lime juice, and butter and mix well until the butter has melted. Add the cream and cinnamon and mix. Return to low to medium heat and simmer for 5 to 10 minutes, stirring constantly until you have a delicious dark caramel. Set aside.

As soon as the cake is done, let it cool in the pan for 10 minutes before cooling on a cooling rack.

Make the buttercream by combining the shortening and cream cheese in a bowl. Beat together then add the confectioners' sugar a few spoons at a time, incorporating slowly to allow the sugar to melt (or you will get a grainy buttercream). Mix in the vanilla.

Pop the frosting into a piping bag and pipe in waves, peaks, or swirls. Drizzle cooled caramel on top, being generous, and your cake is ready to go.

pear and ricotta marble cake

Serves 12	**Prep** 25 minutes
Cook 40 minutes	

This light Italian cake is traditionally made with yogurt, but I make mine with ricotta, which makes it just a little bit (and I mean fractionally) richer. This version is marbled with lemon and chocolate, and each serving has a quarter of a cooked pear to top it off.

Start by quickly but gently cooking the pears (you can use canned pears instead if you want to save time). Pop the pear quarters into a microwaveable dish, add a splash of water, cover with plastic wrap, and cook on high for 4 minutes. As soon as they are done and just soft, drain on some paper towels and set aside.

Preheat the oven to 350°F and generously grease a ring cake pan or a shallower bundt pan—a 9½-inch/24cm or 11-inch/28cm ring pan would be perfect.

Mix the ricotta and sugar together really well. Add the egg yolks, flour, cornstarch, milk, baking powder, and almond extract and mix well to create a smooth cake batter.

For the cake

3 pears, peeled, cored, and quartered (leaving the stalks on)

butter or oil, for greasing the pan

¾ cup + 1 tablespoon/200g ricotta

1½ cups/300g granulated sugar

4 large eggs, separated

2 cups + 6 tablespoons/300g all-purpose flour, sifted

1 tablespoon cornstarch

6 tablespoons/90ml whole milk

1 teaspoon baking powder

1 teaspoon almond extract

1 lemon, finely grated zest only

2 tablespoons cocoa powder, + extra for dusting

Whisk the egg whites to stiff peaks and gently fold the whites a third at a time into the cake batter until you have a much lighter cake batter.

Separate one half of the batter into another bowl. Add the lemon zest to one and the cocoa powder to the other and gently fold them in.

Add the batter to the pan, alternating between the cocoa and lemon until you have finished all the batter, then swirl it all through using a skewer. Put the pear quarters into the pan, stalk side up and leaning onto the edge.

Bake for 40 to 45 minutes. Let cool in the pan for 10 minutes, then gently take out. Once cooled, dust with some cocoa powder and you are ready to eat.

praline king cake

Serves 10   **Prep** 50 minutes, plus rising   **Cook** 40 minutes

For the "cake"

4¾ cups/600g bread flour, + extra for dusting

7 tablespoons/100g unsalted butter, melted and cooled

1 package (2¼ teaspoons/7g fast-acting dried yeast)

1 teaspoon salt

¼ cup/40g granulated sugar

1 cup/240ml whole milk

2 large eggs

butter or cooking oil spray, for greasing the pan

For the praline filling

¼ cup + 2 tablespoons/70g granulated sugar

⅓ cup/40g pecans

8 oz/225g full-fat cream cheese

1 teaspoon vanilla extract

1 teaspoon almond extract

For the icing

1⅔ cups/200g confectioners' sugar, sifted

2–3 tablespoons cold water

To finish

½ cup/50g dried shredded coconut

green and yellow gel food coloring

The clue is in the name here. This is quite some cake, though technically it's more like a sweet bread. It is filled with praline cream and decorated with icing and colored sugar, typically green and yellow. I'm using colored dried shredded coconut instead, but you can stick to sugar if you like your cake super sweet. I've tried the real thing in New Orleans and it's delicious!

Start by making the dough. Put the flour in a mixing bowl with the butter, yeast, salt, and sugar and mix until combined. Make a well in the center. Measure out the milk into a large liquid measuring cup, add the eggs, and whisk just to break up the eggs. If the liquid in the measuring cup does not come up to 1½ cups/350ml, add more milk until it does.

Pour in and mix until the dough comes together. Using a stand mixer with a dough hook, knead for 5 minutes on medium, until the dough is stretchy and elastic. Cover with some plastic wrap and let rise for about 2 hours to double in size.

To make the praline, line a small baking sheet with some parchment paper. Put the sugar in a small pot in an even layer, breaking up any clumps before heating it. Pop onto medium heat and you will see it caramelizing and melting around the edges. As soon as it does, begin mixing and as soon as the sugar has dissolved and is a golden amber, take off the heat. Add the pecans, stir fast, and pour out onto the parchment paper. Allow to set completely. As soon as it has, blitz to rough crumbs in a food processor.

When you are ready to shape the dough, put the cream cheese in a bowl with the vanilla, almond extract, and praline crumble mix and stir really well.

Tip the dough out onto a lightly floured surface and roll out to a 16-inch/40cm square. Take a 2-quart/2-liter bundt pan, the least intricate that you can find, and grease generously with butter or cooking oil spray.

Tip the cream mixture onto the dough and spread an even layer all over, leaving a ½-inch/1cm edge. Roll up like a cinnamon bun. Gently pop in the pan, making sure the seam is touching the inner ring. Pinch the ends together. Cover and let rise until doubled.

When the dough has nearly doubled, preheat the oven to 400°F. Bake for 35 to 40 minutes.

Meanwhile, make the icing by mixing the confectioners' sugar and water until you have a thick icing.

Take the cake out and let cool on a cooling rack. As soon as it is totally cool, pop a baking sheet underneath to catch spillage and drizzle the icing all over the top, allowing it to run freely down the sides.

Divide the dried shredded coconut between two small plastic bags. Pop some different colored food coloring into each one and, using your fingers, massage the coloring in. If you want to avoid using plastic bags, use bowls, using the back of a dessert spoon to work the color into the coconut. Alternating the colors, sprinkle the coconut onto the iced cake.

kouign amann
sugar crunch pastry square

Serves 6   Prep 30 minutes, plus rising and chilling   Cook 45 minutes

2⅓ cups/300g bread flour, + extra for dusting

2 teaspoons fast-acting dried yeast

1 teaspoon salt

¾ cup + 2 tablespoons/ 200ml warm water

2 tablespoons unsalted butter, melted, + extra for greasing the baking sheet

1 cup + 2 tablespoons/ 250g unsalted butter, in a block

½ cup plus 1 tablespoon/ 125g demerara sugar, + extra for sprinkling

1 teaspoon vanilla powder or vanilla bean paste

Kouign amann are delicious yeasted, layered, buttery, sugar-filled parcels from Brittany in France. They are to die for! The first time I had them was about four years ago when my friend Jonny made them, in his lounge pants, while also baking cookies with my kids. I wish he could make them every other weekend for me, but seeing as he has a life and stuff to do, I had to learn to make them myself! In this recipe I've adapted them into one large parcel to cut and share.

To begin, put the flour into the bowl of a stand mixer fitted with a dough hook. Add the yeast to one side of the bowl and the salt to the other.

Now, add the water and melted butter and mix on low speed until it comes together, then turn the mixer up and knead for 6 minutes. If you are doing it by hand, flour the surface lightly and knead until you have a dough that is smooth, stretchy, and elastic. Cover with plastic wrap and let rise until doubled in size.

Sandwich the block of butter between two sheets of plastic wrap and roll out with a rolling pin to a 5½-inch/14cm square. Pop into the fridge and let chill.

Take the dough out and, on a floured surface, roll out to an 8-inch/20cm square. Place the butter in the center of the dough diagonally, so that each side of the butter faces a corner of the dough. Fold the corners of the dough over the butter to enclose it like an envelope. You should have what looks like an X in the middle made by the joining seams.

Roll the dough into an 18 x 6-inch/45 x 15cm rectangle. Fold the bottom third of dough up over the middle third, then fold the top third of the dough over. If you look from the side, you will now have a sandwich of three layers of butter and three layers of dough. Wrap in plastic wrap and place in the fridge for 30 minutes.

Repeat this process twice more, making sure to chill the dough for 30 minutes between folding. Mix the sugar with the vanilla powder or paste. Roll the dough into a rectangle, sprinkle with about half of the vanilla sugar, and fold into thirds again. Working quickly, roll the dough into a large, 12-inch/30cm square. Sprinkle the dough with the remaining vanilla sugar mixture.

Lightly grease a large baking sheet and put the square of pastry straight on.

Take each corner of the pastry and bring into the center of the square, pushing the pastry into the center to keep the dough in place—you should have a beautiful flower shape. Sprinkle with plain demerara sugar and allow to puff up, covered with a sheet of greased plastic wrap, for just 15 minutes.

Preheat the oven to 425°F. Remove the plastic wrap and bake for 40 to 45 minutes, covering with foil half-way through if it begins to brown too much. Remove from the oven and let cool for a couple of minutes before lifting onto a cooling rack.

I love to eat this warm, though it is just as delicious a few hours later. My Achilles' heel, I love this sweet crisp goodness with a cup of tea, on the floor in front of the gas fire, just like I did all those years ago with Jonny and the kids!

cranberry and chile brioche wreath

Serves 8   Prep 40 minutes, plus overnight rising   Cook 20 minutes

4 large eggs

1 tablespoon/20ml whole milk

2¾ cups/350g bread flour, + extra for dusting

1 package (2¼ teaspoons/7g) fast-acting dried yeast

2 tablespoons granulated sugar

1 teaspoon salt

2 teaspoons chile flakes

1¾ cups/200g dried cranberries, chopped

¾ cup + 2 tablespoons/200g unsalted butter, softened and cubed

1 x 9-oz/250g Camembert with a wooden box

To finish

1 egg, lightly beaten

a good pinch of sea salt

2 tablespoons marmalade

Every time my tummy rumbles, I hear it say "bread and cheese, please." I don't ask for much, so usually it's just a very thick slice of brown bread all smothered in butter, too cold out of the fridge, covered by an unevenly sliced slab of cheese. But occasionally I like to fancy things up and, my goodness, is this recipe worth the time! A beautiful wreath of chile-laced brioche balls surround a baked Camembert that's topped with a dollop of marmalade. Expect a flavor explosion of sweet and savory, all soft and oozy, and impossible not to love.

Whisk the eggs and milk in a bowl to incorporate.

In the bowl of a stand mixer, mix the flour, yeast, sugar, and salt until well combined. Add the chile flakes and the cranberries and mix well. Make a well in the center, add the milk mixture and bring the dough roughly together. The mixture will look quite wet and more like a very thick cake batter, but don't worry. Using the stand mixer with the dough hook attached, slowly add the butter to the dough a little at a time until you have used it all up, then knead the dough on high speed for 10 minutes. Cover, pop into the fridge, and let rise overnight.

Next day, line a large baking sheet with some parchment paper. Take the bottom half of the wooden box the cheese comes in and put it in the center of the baking sheet. Put the cheese back in the fridge.

Tip the dough out onto a lightly floured surface and knock the air back. Roll out into a sausage shape and divide into 5 equal pieces. Divide each one into 5, so you have 25 little dough balls. Pinch each ball into the center, turn seam-side down, and roll around in your hand to create a smooth ball. Arrange the first 10 around the wooden cheese box and then the following 15 around them, leaving small gaps to allow them to rise. Cover with some greased plastic wrap and let rise until doubled in size.

Preheat the oven to 375°F. Take the cheese out of the wrapper and pop into the wooden box. Brush the dough balls with the beaten egg and sprinkle all over with a generous helping of salt. Bake for 18 to 20 minutes.

Add spoonfuls of marmalade to the hot cheese and you are ready to eat.

→

middle of the table nut roast

Serves 8–10
Prep 30 minutes, plus cooling **Cook** 1½ hours

1 tablespoon/20g unsalted butter, + extra for greasing the pan

4 cloves of garlic, finely grated

1 red onion, finely diced

2 tablespoons tomato paste

7 oz/200g button mushrooms, finely chopped

1 large carrot, grated (about 1⅓ cups/150g)

1 teaspoon salt

1 teaspoon chile powder

1 teaspoon ground cumin

½ teaspoon ground turmeric

¾ cup/150g red split lentils

1⅔ cups/400ml vegetable stock

1 cup/100g fine dried breadcrumbs

1½ cups/150g mixed nuts, finely chopped

3 large eggs, lightly beaten

3½ oz/100g mature Cheddar cheese, finely grated

a small handful of fresh cilantro, finely chopped

For the flavor glaze

1 tablespoon Marmite or Vegemite

1 tablespoon hot water

1 tablespoon ketchup

For a long time I had a preconceived notion that a nut roast couldn't be yummy, because it was a replacement for meatloaf, but recently I realized how wrong I was. A nut roast shouldn't be seen as a substitute or replacement, but as the centerpiece to your meal, sitting proud, pretty, and delicious for everyone to enjoy! This is the kind of thing that if not finished can be eaten cold and sliced the next day, with a salad or—the way I like to eat it—sandwiched between a heavily buttered, overly floured bun, the size of my head, with the biggest squirt of steak sauce!

Preheat the oven to 350°F. Lightly grease and line an 8½ x 4½-inch/900g loaf pan.

Pop the butter into a large nonstick pan and heat until melted, then add the garlic and cook for a few seconds until just golden. Add the onion and cook for another 5 minutes, until just soft.

Add the tomato paste, mushrooms, carrot, and salt and cook for another 5 minutes. Now add all the spices and cook for 5 minutes. Add the lentils and stock and cook on low to medium heat for 15 minutes, until the lentils are softened and all the liquid has evaporated from the pan.

Take the mixture off the heat, transfer to a large bowl, and let cool for at least 30 minutes. As soon as it is cool enough to touch, add the breadcrumbs, nuts, eggs, cheese, and cilantro and give it all a thorough mix until you have a really colorful mixture that is quite stiff.

Spoon the mixture into the prepped pan and push down using the back of a spoon, making sure to pack it in tightly. Bake for 50 minutes to 1 hour, then let cool in the pan for 20 minutes before turning out into a small roasting dish.

Turn the broiler on. Mix the Marmite with the hot water so you have a mixture that is runny enough to brush, then add the ketchup. Brush the outside of the nut roast with the mixture and broil for just 3 to 5 minutes and your nut roast is ready to serve.

kransekake cookie tower

| Serves 16 |
| Prep 1 hour, plus chilling |
| Cook 40 minutes |

For the cookie dough

5¼ cups/500g almond meal

4 cups/500g confectioners' sugar, sifted

4 large egg whites

1 teaspoon almond extract

vegetable oil, for greasing the pan

For the icing

3 tablespoons water or lemon juice

3¼ cups/400g confectioners' sugar, sifted

2 large egg whites

1 tablespoon black sesame seeds

To finish

chocolate-covered nuts, seeds, and wrapped chocolates

sugared almonds and edible flowers (or other edible decorations)

This is a Scandinavian cookie tower that is traditionally created for special celebrations and, boy, is it special, with its rings of chewy, sweet, almond cookie dough, stacked one on top of the other. Specialty recipes often require specialty equipment, but I have found a way of making this without needing anything fancier than a round cake tin pan, a knife, and the ability to cut a free-hand circle.

Begin by toasting the almond meal to really bring out its nutty flavor. Toast in a nonstick pan over medium heat, stirring all the time, until golden. Let cool totally and then sift to remove any lumps. Add the confectioners' sugar and stir until well combined.

Make a well in the center, add the egg whites and almond extract, and mix until you have a dough that comes together. If you find it's a bit crumbly, add a few drops of water until it does. Roll the dough into a flat patty, wrap, and chill for at least 2 hours.

→

Grease and line the bottom of a 10-inch/25cm springform pan. Take the dough out and place in the pan. Using your hands or the bottom of a heavy tumbler, push the dough in until you have a smooth, even layer that covers the bottom right to the edges. Remove the side of the pan, then measure a rim, ½-inch/1.5cm inward from the outside of the circle, and score a circle. Do the same again, creating another ring and then another, and so on, until you have a small circle in the center. You should have 7 rings and 1 circle.

Preheat the oven to 400°F. Line three baking sheets (or as many as you have) with some parchment paper.

Gently lift away the outside ring of cookie. Pop onto a baking sheet. If the shape gets lost, you can just fix it or, if it breaks, just push it back together. Do this to all of the rings.

Bake for 10 minutes for the large rings, 6 to 8 minutes for the medium rings, and 4 to 6 minutes for the small rings. They should be golden and will be very soft, so let cool on the sheets for 5 to 10 minutes, then transfer to a wire rack to cool completely. Do this until you have baked them all.

Make the icing by combining the lemon juice or water and the confectioners' sugar in a bowl and mixing with the egg whites. This is the type of icing that will set hard and not run everywhere—perfect for piping. Pop the icing into a piping bag, snip off a small opening, and, starting with the biggest ring, pipe back and forth across the width of the ring, going all the way around. Sprinkle with the black sesame seeds as quickly as possible before the icing starts to dry. Repeat for the other rings.

It's time to stack. Take the largest ring and pipe icing on the serving board or dish so you can "glue" the ring in place. Pop the next ring on top, using a few drops of icing to glue it, and keep doing this until you've done about three rings. Now fill the hollow in the middle with some of your chocolate-covered nuts or sweets. Add a few more rings, and again fill the middle with nuts or sweets. This cake is not traditionally filled, but I like the idea that the otherwise empty cavity is a receptacle for even more sweet delights.

Once you get to the top, secure the last piece with icing. I like to decorate with edible flowers, sugared almonds, or other edible decorations, whatever the occasion calls for.

chapter six

COOKIES

& BITES

———

raspberry amaretti cookies

> **Makes** about 20 **Prep** 40 minutes
> **Cook** 15 minutes

butter, for greasing the baking sheets

4 large egg whites

1¾ cups/340g granulated sugar

3½ cups/340g almond meal

⅔ oz/18g freeze-dried raspberries, blitzed to a powder

1 teaspoon almond extract

20 small fresh raspberries (or see headnote)

¾ cup/100g confectioners' sugar

Amaretti are a cookie that people seem slightly afraid to make. Just because they are often found for sale in beautiful tins with crunchy cellophane and fancy bows doesn't mean they are difficult or tricky to create at home. In fact, homemade amaretti are the best, these ones in particular, which are soft and delicious and almondy, with a subtle hint of raspberry all the way through and a hidden raspberry in the center. These too can be given as a gift. Just remind your recipients that the cookies should be eaten straightaway because of the fresh fruit. If you want these to last longer, you can use freeze-dried raspberries instead of fresh.

Start by preheating the oven to 375°F and lining two large baking sheets with parchment paper, greasing them just very slightly to allow the paper to stick to the sheet and not go flying.

Now get on to making the cookie paste mixture by whisking the egg whites in a large clean bowl until they are firm. Add the sugar and fold it in gently using a spatula or metal spoon. Add the almond meal along with the blitzed-up raspberry powder and almond extract and mix thoroughly until you have an even paste.

Have the confectioners' sugar at the ready along with the raspberries. Take a heaped tablespoon of mixture, about 1½ oz/40g if you want to be precise, and shape it into a flat round disc. Wrap the disc around a raspberry to form a ball shape, pinching it together underneath so that the raspberry is completely enclosed. The paste may crack a bit along the top, but don't worry. Repeat with the rest of the cookie paste.

Drop each ball into the confectioners' sugar and roll around until fully and generously coated. Place seam-side down on the baking sheets, making sure they are about ¾ inch/2cm apart, as they will spread just a little.

Now bake these for 12 to 15 minutes, until they are just lightly golden. Take them out and let cool on the sheet for 10 minutes before moving them to a cooling rack.

rhubarb and custard butter kisses

Makes about 20 **Prep** 40 minutes
Cook 12 minutes

The classic rhubarb and custard hard candies don't actually taste much like rhubarb, but they are certainly distinct and unique in flavor, so I thought it would be interesting to mix them with melted white chocolate for the filling to my delicate rippled custard cookies.

Have two baking sheets at the ready, lined with some parchment paper and lightly greased.

To make the dough, combine the butter, confectioners' sugar, and vanilla seeds in a bowl and beat until the mixture is really light and fluffy. Add the flour, custard powder, and baking powder and mix until it all comes together nicely into a thick paste.

Add the food coloring to a corner of the paste and mix the paste carefully in that corner so you are coloring only a quarter. Take a clean spoon and mix the whole thing so you have uneven ripple throughout.

For the cookies

¾ cup + 2 tablespoons/ 200g unsalted butter, + extra for greasing the baking sheets

6 tablespoons/50g confectioners' sugar

½ vanilla pod, with the seeds scraped out

1⅔ cups/200g all-purpose flour, sifted

4 teaspoons custard powder

½ teaspoon baking powder

2 drops of pink gel food coloring

For the filling

5¼ oz/150g white chocolate, chopped or chips

1½ oz/40g rhubarb and custard candies

Preheat the oven to 375°F.

Attach a medium ½-inch/1.25cm open star-tip nozzle to a piping bag and gently add all the mixture. Pipe 1½-inch/4cm star shapes onto the prepared paper, leaving a ¾-inch/2cm gap in between each, as these do spread a little. Bake for 10 to 12 minutes, then let cool completely on the sheet.

Make the filling by melting the chocolate and setting it aside. Crush the candies to crumbs. I crush them so they are mostly fine with a few slightly larger pieces, but you don't want too many large pieces or the cookies won't sandwich together.

Once the cookies are cool, turn them over so you have the flat bottoms exposed. Take a very small spoonful of the melted chocolate and spread on the underside of each cookie. Sprinkle the crushed candies onto half the cookies and then take the other cookies and pop straight on top. Arrange on the sheet and place in a cool spot for the chocolate to set, then they are totally ready to eat.

chocolate, hazelnut, and rosemary ladies' kisses

> **Makes** 23   **Prep** 30 minutes, plus chilling and setting   **Cook** 15 minutes (20 minutes if roasting the hazelnuts)

For the cookies

⅔ cup/100g chopped roasted hazelnuts

¾ cup/100g all-purpose flour

7 tablespoons/85g granulated sugar

7 tablespoons/100g unsalted butter, + extra for greasing the baking sheets

For the filling

3½ oz/100g dark chocolate, chopped or chips

1 tablespoon dried rosemary

These are the sweetest little Italian cookies I have ever eaten. I first tried them at an Italian restaurant, where they were just too inviting not to have one . . . and when I say one, I most definitely mean ten! The cookies are flavored with hazelnuts, then sandwiched with a dark chocolate that I like to lift with a little dried rosemary.

Pop the hazelnuts into a food processor. I like to buy the pre-roasted chopped ones, but if you can't find them you can roast the hazelnuts in a dry nonstick frying pan until golden, then let cool completely before blitzing to fine crumbs. Then, to save on washing up, make the entire dough in the processor.

Add the flour, sugar, and butter and whiz until a dough starts to come together in the machine. As soon as it does, take out, wrap in plastic wrap, and chill for at least 1 hour so the dough can firm up.

Line and very lightly grease two baking sheets.

Get the dough out of the fridge and take pinches of it, measuring exactly 0.28 oz/8g each. I know this seems pedantic, and normally I'm not too bothered about being exact, but because here two cookies are sandwiched together, it's important to make sure they are the same size. Roll each pinch of dough into a ball and pop onto the sheets, evenly spaced out.

Put back in the fridge and chill for another 1 hour.

Preheat the oven to 350°F.

Bake the cookies for 12 to 15 minutes, until they are just lightly golden brown. Take them out and let cool completely on a rack. As soon as they are cooled, get on to that filling.

Melt the chocolate either in a bowl over a simmering pot of water or in the microwave, my preferred option for such a small amount. As soon as the chocolate is smooth and glossy, mix in the dried rosemary. The warm chocolate will activate that dried herb and bring it back to life in all its fragrant, herby glory.

Take one cookie and dollop the smallest amount of the chocolate in the center of the flat underside. Too much and it will spill over and you won't get that clean line in the center. Pop another cookie on top of the chocolate, gluing them together. Do the same to the rest.

Allow the chocolate to set for at least half an hour before eating. These can last a few months in an airtight jar—assuming you don't eat them all at once!

speculoos spiced cookies and crunchy spread

Makes 25 Prep 40 minutes, plus chilling Cook 15 minutes

For the speculoos spice mix

4 x 1¼-oz/34g jars of ground cinnamon

1 x 1½-oz/42g jar of ground nutmeg

1 x 1¼-oz/35g jar of ground cloves

1 x 1¼-oz/33g jar of ground black pepper

1 x 1-oz/28g jar of ground ginger

¾ oz/20g star anise, crushed to a fine powder (optional)

For the cookies

6 tablespoons/85g unsalted butter, softened, + extra for greasing the baking sheets

¾ cup/150g brown sugar

1¼ cups/155g all-purpose flour, sifted, + extra for dusting

4 teaspoons speculoos spice mix

½ teaspoon baking powder

a pinch of salt

For the crunchy spread

2 tablespoons brown sugar

1 teaspoon speculoos spice mix

7 tablespoons/100ml condensed milk

1 tablespoon unsalted butter, softened

1 teaspoon lemon juice

4½ oz/125g speculoos cookies, this is about 7 or 8 cookies

My dad used to give these cookies to customers at his restaurant, individually wrapped and propped on the side of their coffee. I'm not big on ginger cookies, so these are my alternative: dark, crisp, and spiced but not exclusively with ginger. If you're going to the trouble of making them, I highly recommend you make the spread too—it's so easy and a total must! This recipe produces a big batch of the special spice mix, but as it is so unique in flavor and not always easy to buy except at Christmas or in the Netherlands, I like to make plenty. It can be used wherever you want a spicy hit: in crumbles, cakes, buttercream, smoothies, oatmeal, French toast, the list goes on and on.

Start by mixing all the speculoos spice mix ingredients straight into a large jar so you are ready to spice anything you want with this wonderfully special blend of spices.

Put the butter in a bowl along with the brown sugar. This sugar is so important to the cookie dough, not just for the deep caramel color, but also for the dark caramel flavor. Beat this mixture until it is slightly fluffy and airy and a lot paler than when you first started.

Now add the flour, along with the spice mix, the baking powder, and the salt and mix until you have formed a dough. If you find you have still got stray bits of flour that just won't come together and the dough is a little dry, then add a few drops of water at a time until the dough comes together. Wrap the dough in some plastic wrap and flatten into a rough rectangle shape (this will help with rolling later). Let chill in the fridge for at least 1 hour.

Preheat the oven to 375°F and line two baking sheets with some parchment paper, greasing them very slightly so that they stick to the sheets without flying everywhere.

Once the dough is out, lightly flour the worktop and roll out the dough to a 12½ x 7½-inch/32.5 x 20cm rectangle, just under ¼ inch/5mm thick. Have one of the shorter ends closest to you. Now use a fluted knife, a kid's fluted play-dough cutter, or just a knife to cut it vertically into 1½-inch/4cm-wide strips. Cut the strips into 2½-inch/6.5cm-long cookies. So we are dividing the rectangle into 25 cookies by making 4 vertical cuts at 1½-inch/4cm intervals and 4 horizontal cuts at 2½-inch/6.5cm intervals.

Once you have your rectangles cut, pop them onto the sheets about ¾ inch/2cm apart, giving them some room to spread. Bake for 14 to 16 minutes, until they are just slightly darker around the edges. Let them cool completely on the sheet before eating, dipping, and transferring to an airtight cookie jar.

If you are making the spread, which I highly recommend, pop the sugar, spice mix, condensed milk, butter, and lemon juice into a small food processor and whiz until you have a smooth paste. Add the cookies and whiz until you have the crunch just as you like it. Spoon into a jar, place in the fridge, and it will last in there for up to 1 month.

pressed flower shortbread shards

1 cup + 2 tablespoons/
250g unsalted butter,
softened

½ cup/110g granulated
sugar, + extra for
dusting

¾ cup + 2 tablespoons/
360g all-purpose flour

semolina, for dusting

a small handful of mixed
herbs and edible flowers
(depending on what
you can find or have
growing)

Makes 30 shards   **Prep** 40 minutes,
plus chilling   **Cook** 30 minutes, plus
15 minutes resting

In my opinion, shortbread rarely needs much in terms of improvement. It is a wonderful and delicious thing of buttery beauty. But if we're going to fancy it up, here is a simple and very beautiful way of doing so, especially if you have edible flowers and herbs growing in your garden.

Beat the butter and sugar in a bowl until it is really smooth and quite light and fluffy. Add the flour and gently fold it in until you have a smooth dough, using a rubber spatula, and then get your hands in to form one lump of dough.

Take the dough and wrap in some plastic wrap, flatten it, and chill in the fridge for 1 hour.

Once the dough has chilled, take out and tear off two large sheets of plastic wrap. Put the dough in the center of one sheet and the other sheet on top. Roll out until it is a 14 x 12-inch/35 x 30cm rectangle, about ¼ inch/5mm thick.

Have a large baking sheet ready with some parchment paper and sprinkle generously with semolina.

Take off the top layer of the plastic wrap and, using the other sheet, turn the dough out onto the semolina layer. Pull the plastic wrap off. Now gently push the flowers and herbs into the dough. Place a sheet of parchment paper on top and roll gently to push the flowers in securely. Put another baking sheet on top and put back into the fridge for 30 minutes to firm up.

Preheat the oven to 325°F.

Put the sheet (with the other sheet still on top) into the oven to bake for 30 minutes. As soon as it is done, remove and let cool like this for 15 minutes.

Now take the sheet off the top and pull off the paper to reveal the beautiful flowers and herbs. Using a serrated knife, and while the dough is still warm, cut into shards and let cool completely.

Once cool it should be crisp and delicious and ready to eat—if you can bear to eat something so pretty, though that never stopped me!

black sesame seed snacks

Makes approx. 50 (and 5 cups of masala chai)
Prep 20 minutes plus chilling (10 minutes for the chai)   Cook 15 minutes (1 hour for the chai)

For the snacks

3 cups/375g all-purpose flour, + extra for dusting

1 teaspoon salt

¼ cup/50g granulated sugar

4 teaspoons black sesame seeds

7 tablespoons/100ml cold water

2 large eggs, lightly beaten

6 tablespoons/50g confectioners' sugar

For the masala chai mix

3 x 1¼-oz/34g jars of ground cinnamon

1 x 1-oz/28g jar of ground ginger

1 x 1-oz/32g jar of ground nutmeg

1 x 1-oz/26g jar of cardamom pods, seeds removed and crushed to a powder (unless you can find ground)

1 x 1¼-oz/35g jar of ground cloves

1 x 1 oz/25g jar of ground black pepper

For the tea

1 tablespoon masala chai mix

1 quart/1 liter whole milk

5 black tea bags

condensed milk, to serve

These are very similar to traditional snacks called nimki, which are technically savory though I love them dusted in loads of confectioners' sugar—they can be whatever you want them to be: sweet, savory, or anything in between. I always eat these with a hot cup of masala chai.

To make the snacks, combine the flour, salt, and sugar in a large bowl with the black sesame seeds and mix well. Make a well in the center, add the water and eggs, and bring the dough together using a rubber spatula, then get your hands in to form a soft dough that is somewhere between a firmer bread dough and softer cookie one.

Flatten it to a square about 1-inch/2.5cm thick, wrap in plastic wrap, and chill in the fridge for at least 1 hour to allow the dough to rest. Meanwhile, preheat the oven to 375°F and line two baking sheets with parchment paper.

Take the dough out of the fridge, put on a floured surface, and roll out to a ¼-inch/5mm thickness. Using a 2-inch/5cm round cutter, cut out circles, putting them onto the lined sheets as you go. Re-roll and cut the scraps until you have used up all the dough.

Bake in the oven for 10 to 12 minutes until light golden brown on the bottom, being careful not to overbake as they will harden. Let cool on the sheet then tip into an airtight jar. Add the confectioners' sugar and toss gently like the drum of a washing machine to allow the sugar to coat them. Store in the jar ready to eat.

For the masala chai, first make up the mix and store in a large jar. You will have lots, so be adventurous. It's not just for tea; you can spice up all sorts of things, such as cookies, cakes, oatmeal, and smoothies.

For the tea, put 1 tablespoon of the spice mix into a pot with the milk and tea bags and bring to a boil. Let simmer on the lowest heat for 1 hour with the lid on. The tea should be strong and rich.

Before serving add 1 to 2 tablespoons of condensed milk to each cup. Strain the tea into a clean pot to remove some of the spice mix and the tea bags, then pour the tea into each cup, making sure to stir, and that is your masala chai—plus you have enough of the spice mix left for when you want some more!

chewy chocolate-chip cookies

Makes 23   Prep 20 minutes, plus chilling
Cook 15 minutes per batch (dough balls can be frozen and baked for 20 minutes from frozen)

1 cup/225g unsalted butter

3¼ cups/400g all-purpose flour

¾ teaspoon baking powder

¾ teaspoon baking soda

½ teaspoon salt

12 oz/340g milk chocolate, chopped or chips

scant 1 cup/200g brown sugar

¾ cup/150g granulated sugar

2 large eggs

2 large egg yolks

1 teaspoon vanilla extract

1 teaspoon almond extract

sea salt flakes, for sprinkling

These days you can satisfy your sweet/savory tooth as quickly as heading to the supermarket or simply dialing and ordering to your doorstep. Instant gratification has its place, but there is a joy in making something from scratch even if you can buy it from anywhere. Making a deliciously chewy, perfectly rounded, choc-chip cookie is one of life's joys, whether it's for yourself, a bake sale, baking with little ones, a distraction, or just to fill a Sunday morning. So these are joy on a baking sheet!

Start by melting the butter either in a small pot or in a medium bowl in the microwave. Let cool.

In another bowl, combine the flour, baking powder, baking soda, and salt and mix until well combined. Add the chocolate chips and mix again.

Add the sugars, eggs, egg yolks, vanilla, and almond extract to the melted butter and give the whole thing a really good mix until well combined.

Make a well in the center of the dry ingredients and then pour in the liquid ingredients. Mix until you have a stiff dough and the chocolate is well distributed. Chill in the fridge for 30 minutes.

Take a baking sheet lined with parchment paper and divide the mixture into balls of about 2 oz/60g each. I'm not really into being totally exact with every cookie looking identical, but something about uniform cookies pleases me, so it's worth measuring them out. Once you have done them all, cover with some plastic wrap.

The hardest bit now is chilling them. You have to chill them for at least 4 hours, but I would recommend chilling them totally overnight.

When you are ready to bake, line two baking sheets with parchment paper and preheat the oven to 350°F. Place about six dough balls on each sheet, making sure to space them around 2 inches/5cm apart to allow room to spread. Sprinkle a little sea salt on each dough ball and bake for 14 to 16 minutes. You'll know these are ready when they are just very lightly golden brown around the edges and paler in the center—that's the softer, chewy bit, my favorite part!

You want to let these cool on the sheets for at least 10 minutes before transferring them to a rack, then using the sheets to bake the remaining cookies.

coffee meringue bark

Makes 2 large sheets   Prep 20 minutes
Cook 1 hour

butter, for greasing
the baking sheets

2 large eggs, separated

½ cup + 2 tablespoons/
125g granulated sugar

2 teaspoons instant
coffee

2 teaspoons hot water

2 teaspoons black
sesame seeds

This gluten-free sweet treat is really easy to make. What I love is that you can play around with flavors, toppings, and gel colorings to change it up, though I've kept this version fairly simple. Easy to store and equally as easy to eat, this bark doubles up as a quick decoration for cakes or cupcakes.

Put the egg whites in a large, grease-free bowl and have ½ cup/100g of the sugar ready.

Preheat the oven to 300°F. Line two baking sheets with parchment paper and lightly grease.

Put the egg yolks in a small bowl along with the remaining 2 tablespoons/25g of the sugar. Put the instant coffee in another small bowl with the hot water and mix. Add to the egg yolk mixture and set aside.

Using electric beaters or a stand mixer if you have one, begin whisking the egg whites until really foamy. As soon as they increase in volume, start adding the sugar a small spoonful at a time, whisking for at least 10 seconds between each addition. It's really important that all the sugar crystals dissolve so the bark doesn't leak. After each addition, stop and scrape down the sides to get any stray sugar crystals. Do this until you have stiff peaks that are glossy and shiny.

Now, beat the coffee and egg yolk mixture until it is glossy, shiny, and smooth and quadrupled in size. This mixture should be really thick, but not so stiff that it will not run off the beaters.

Divide the egg white mixture between the two sheets, spreading really thin to a 12-inch/30cm square. Drizzle the coffee mixture all over the egg whites, then sprinkle with the sesame seeds.

Bake for 1 hour, which will give it lots of time to dry out and create a really good snap. Once the time is up, let cool completely. As soon as it's totally cooled, snap into shards and pop into an airtight container where they will happily keep. Meringue bark loses its snap if left out on a humid day, so make sure to get it into that airtight container once cool.

ginger and almond florentines

¼ cup/50g unsalted butter, + extra for greasing the baking sheets

¼ cup/50g brown sugar

2 tablespoons golden syrup or light corn syrup

6 tablespoons/50g all-purpose flour

2½ oz/75g crystallized ginger, finely chopped

½ cup/50g sliced almonds

1 orange, finely grated zest only

7 oz/200g dark chocolate

2⅓ oz/65g white chocolate

Makes 18   **Prep** 25 minutes, plus setting
Cook 15 minutes

Brandy snap meets cookie meets toffee, these are delicious to have lying around the house for a sweet treat, but even better wrapped and given away as a present. Laced with chopped crystallized ginger, sliced almonds, and a hint of orange zest, they're finally dipped in chocolate to add to the party in your mouth!

Start by preheating the oven to 400°F. Line and very lightly grease three baking sheets.

To make the florentines (and these are so easy I think you will be making them again), place the butter and sugar in a medium pot along with the golden syrup and heat until the sugar has dissolved and there are no more granules.

Take off the heat and add the flour, ginger, almonds, and zest and mix to thoroughly combine.

Take small spoonfuls of the mixture and pop six equal mounds on each sheet, leaving plenty of room for them to spread. Bake for 6 to 8 minutes. As soon as they are light golden in the center and just slightly darker on the outside, they are ready to take out. They are still fragile when very hot, so will need to rest for about 5 minutes before you even think about moving them.

Have a cooling rack ready and gently, using an offset spatula, take them one by one to cool on the rack. Once they have cooled completely they are ready to dip. Now, traditionally they have one side covered in chocolate, but that doesn't agree with me—where am I supposed to hold it without getting melted chocolate all over my fingers? So I like to half dip. No messy fingers and I get to taste the florentines two different ways.

So, melt the chocolates in separate bowls. Make sure to put the dark chocolate in a bowl deep enough for dipping the florentines. Add the melted white chocolate directly on top of the melted dark chocolate, then use a skewer to create swirls.

Take each round and dip half in, then pop out and let set on the sheet with the parchment paper that they baked on initially. Allow the chocolate to set and they are ready to eat!

→

fennel and coconut breadsticks

½ cup/40g dried shredded coconut, + 3 tablespoons for sprinkling

3½ cups/450g bread flour, + extra for dusting

1 package (2¼ teaspoons/ 7g) fast-acting dried yeast

1 teaspoon salt

2 teaspoons fennel seeds, lightly crushed

1 cup/240ml warm water (you may need a splash more)

vegetable oil, for greasing the plastic wrap

1 egg white mixed with 1 tablespoon water

1 teaspoon sea salt flakes

Makes 12   **Prep** 25 minutes, plus rising
Cook 20 minutes

Yes, you can buy breadsticks anywhere, but they are easy to make too, especially if you want to vary the flavors. I find making them very therapeutic—and then you get to eat your therapy. I can't think of a better way to feel chilled. These are dotted with fennel and covered with coconut. I love that they are both sweet and savory at the same time, so you can eat them dipped in peanut butter, chocolate spread, tomato jam, or onion chutney! Delicious all around.

Dust two large baking sheets with the dried shredded coconut.

Put the flour, yeast, salt, and crushed fennel seeds into a large bowl and mix to combine. Make a well in the center, add the water, and bring the dough together using a rubber spatula. Now get your hands in and mix to get a dough ball.

Knead well for 10 minutes by hand on a lightly floured work surface or for 5 minutes if using a stand mixer fitted with a dough hook on high speed.

Divide the mixture into 12 equal portions, about 2 oz/60g each if we're being precise. Take each ball and roll into a long sausage shape, about 10 inches/ 25cm long, on a very lightly floured surface. What I love about making these is the unevenness of the breadsticks—they all have the odd nodule or quirk that makes them extra special. So yes, we want them to be the same, but do we really?

Place the breadsticks on the prepared baking sheets, spacing them 1 inch/2.5 cm apart. Cover loosely with a sheet of greased plastic wrap and let rise in a warm place until they have doubled in size.

Meanwhile, preheat the oven to 425°F.

Remove the plastic wrap and brush the breadsticks with the egg white mixed with water. Sprinkle with the sea salt flakes and then the coconut and bake in the top part of the oven for 10 minutes. Cover the sheets with foil to prevent the coconut from burning and bake for another 10 minutes, until golden and the coconut on the bottom and top of the breadsticks is toasted golden.

Take out and let cool completely on the sheet before eating with your chosen dip.

spicy chickpea crispbreads

3¼ cups/300g chickpea flour, sifted, + a little extra for dusting

2 teaspoons chile flakes

1 teaspoon paprika

1 teaspoon salt

½ teaspoon baking powder

2 tablespoons ghee or butter, softened

1 teaspoon honey

⅓ cup/85ml cold water (you may need a little more)

1 egg white mixed with 1 tablespoon cold water

2 teaspoons cumin seeds

1 teaspoon curry powder

Makes about 30 shards   **Prep** 20 minutes
Cook 20 minutes

I grew up watching my mum, very not British, eating spicy snacks with her tea. I never understood until I started drinking teas and realized how well the two go together, especially if your tea is sweet and your snack is savory. These spicy crispbreads do not have to be eaten with tea; they are just as great used as a vehicle for cheese or chutney or instead of poppadoms. But they do work brilliantly just with a cup of tea.

Start by preheating the oven to 400°F and having two baking sheets at the ready.

Put the sifted chickpea flour into a bowl. It's important, as chickpea flour has a little more moisture in it than regular flour, so is more prone to large clumps. Now add the chile flakes, paprika, salt, and baking powder and mix well to combine.

Add the ghee or butter along with the honey, and, using your hands, mix and crumble the butter in until you have no large lumps left. Make a well in the center and add the cold water. Using a rubber spatula, mix the dough until it starts coming together. Now it's time to get your hands in and give everything a really good squeeze to bring the dough together into

a neat ball. The dough should be quite firm, but, if you find it is still quite dry, add a few teaspoons of water at a time until the dough comes together.

Divide the dough in two. Dust the work surface with a little of the chickpea flour and start gently rolling out half of the dough.

Now take a large sheet of parchment paper, the right size to fit the baking sheets, pop the dough on top of that, and roll on that paper. This will just mean transferring will be easier. Roll as thin as possible, about 1/16 inch/1.5mm thick, making sure to dust your rolling pin if you need to.

Pop onto the sheet. Repeat with the other half of the dough, putting it on the second baking sheet once rolled out. Poke the dough all over with a fork at this stage to reduce bubbling during baking.

Mix the egg white with the water, brush all over the dough, and sprinkle with the cumin seeds and the curry powder. Bake for 16 to 18 minutes, until the center of the crispbread is dry to touch.

As soon as the crispbreads come out of the oven, let them cool on the sheets until they have cooled completely, giving them loads of room to dry and crisp up some more. Take the dried crispbreads, break up into shards, and they are ready to eat any which way.

mint choc-chip nanaimo bars

Makes 16 bars (and 2 milkshakes)
Prep 25 minutes, plus chilling
(10 minutes for the milkshakes)
Cook 5 minutes

For the cookie base

- ½ cup + 1 tablespoon/ 125g unsalted butter, + extra for greasing the pan
- ¼ cup/50g granulated sugar
- ½ cup/40g cocoa powder
- 1 large egg, lightly whisked
- 7 oz/200g graham crackers, crushed
- 1 cup/100g dried shredded coconut
- ⅓ cup/50g almonds, roughly chopped

For the mint topping

- 7 tablespoons/100g unsalted butter, softened
- 2 tablespoons whole milk
- 2 cups/250g confectioners' sugar, sifted
- a few drops of mint extract
- a few drops of green food coloring
- 6 after-dinner chocolate mints, roughly chopped or broken

For the milkshake

- 2 squares of Nanaimo
- 2 scoops of vanilla ice cream
- a small handful of fresh mint
- 1¼ cups/300ml whole milk
- chocolate sauce
- whipped cream
- chocolate chips or shavings
- 2 sprigs of fresh mint

When planning any vacation, the first thing I look at is places to eat. My kids love to do this too. When we decided to travel through Canada, we immediately went online and searched "Things to eat in Canada." There was a wealth of foods, but Nanaimo bars really stuck out. These have a rich chocolate base and a sweet mint custard with choc chips, because the word mint should always be followed with the words choc chip! These also make a delicious milkshake. Just saying . . .

Line a 9-inch/23cm baking pan with parchment paper and lightly grease.

Combine the butter, sugar, and cocoa powder in a medium saucepan and heating gently until the butter has melted and the sugar has dissolved. Take off the heat and let cool for 10 minutes. Now add the egg and quickly mix until quite thick. Add the graham crackers, coconut, and almonds and mix until everything is well coated. Put into the lined pan and press into an even layer. Pop into the fridge for 30 minutes.

Make the topping by combining the butter and milk in a bowl and beating well. Add the confectioners' sugar and combine using a spoon, then go back in with the beaters and beat until really light and fluffy. Add the mint extract and enough food coloring to achieve that minty color. Finally, add the after-dinner mints and fold them in so they are evenly dispersed.

Spread the mint mixture evenly on top of the chilled base and chill in the fridge for another 30 minutes. Take out, cut into squares, and these are ready to eat.

To make the milkshake, put 2 Nanaimo bars in a blender with the ice cream, mint, and milk and whiz until thick. Squeeze the chocolate sauce down the inside edge of two tall glasses and pour in the milkshake. Top with some whipped cream, chocolate chips or shavings, and then a sprig of mint. You are set!

chapter seven

BREADS
& BUNS

cornish splits

Makes 9   Prep 30 minutes, plus rising   Cook 25 minutes

For the loaves

3 cups/375g bread flour, + extra for dusting

2 tablespoons unsalted butter, softened, + extra for greasing

1 package (2¼ teaspoons/7g) fast-acting dried yeast

2 teaspoons granulated sugar

¼ teaspoon salt

1¼ cups/300ml warm milk

For the quick jam

14 oz/400g frozen strawberries, defrosted

½ cup/100g granulated sugar

1 lime, finely grated zest and juice

2 teaspoons cornstarch

For the filling

1⅔ cups/400ml heavy cream

2 tablespoons confectioners' sugar, + 1 extra tablespoon for dusting

1 teaspoon vanilla extract

butter, for spreading

These glorious little delights are the kind of things that make me remember why I love food—because often the simplest recipes can be the most delicious. These round, yeasted loaves are split while still warm, buttered generously, filled with strawberry jam, and then served with the biggest dollop of freshly whipped vanilla-laced cream! What could be better? In my mind, nothing.

Start by making the dough. Pop the flour into a bowl, add the butter, and rub in until there are no more lumps. Add the yeast and sugar to one side of the bowl and then the salt to the other side.

Make a well in the center and add the warm milk. Using a rubber spatula, mix the whole thing until it just comes together.

Now it's time to knead. This dough is super sticky, so this is definitely better done in a stand mixer, if you have one, using the dough hook on medium speed for 6 minutes. If you are using your hands, make sure to dust the surface and your hands with flour, and re-flour them whenever the dough feels too sticky. Then work that dough, kneading it for about 10 minutes, until it is smooth and elastic. Let rise in a warm spot until it has doubled in size.

Meanwhile, make the quick jam. Put the strawberries in a pot with the sugar. Add the zest of the lime. Squeeze the lime juice into a small bowl, add the cornstarch, and mix to a paste. Add to the pot and mix well. Put the pot on medium heat and cook for about 5 minutes, stirring occasionally, until the mixture has thickened. Take off the heat and set aside to cool completely.

Once the dough has doubled in size, take out of the bowl and drop onto a floured surface.

Roll the dough into a sausage shape and cut into 9 equal pieces. If you want to be precise, then each one needs to be about 2¾ oz/80g.

Pop the loaves onto a lightly greased baking sheet, cover with a piece of greased plastic wrap, and let rise until doubled in size.

→

Preheat the oven to 400°F.

Bake the loaves for 15 minutes. As soon as they are done, remove the sheet from the oven, place the buns on a cooling rack, and let cool completely.

While the loaves cool, mix the cream in a large bowl with the confectioners' sugar and vanilla, whip up to soft peaks, then spoon it into a piping bag.

Once the loaves have cooled, it's time to do the "split" bit of the Cornish splits. Cut each bun on a slant, starting at the top and cutting downward on an angle, being sure not to go all the way through or you will have a Cornish burger!

Butter the inside of each bun generously on the bottom half, spoon in some of that cooled jam, and then pipe in the cream.

Dust with a little confectioners' sugar and eat straightaway. No hanging around here!

cinnamon and cocoa swirl loaf

Makes 1 loaf
Prep 35 minutes, plus rising
Cook 30 minutes

For the bread

4 cups/500g bread flour, + extra for dusting

2 teaspoons ground cinnamon

2 teaspoons salt

1 package (2¼ teaspoons /7g) fast-acting dried yeast

3 tablespoons oil, + extra for greasing

1¼ cups/300ml lukewarm water

For the swirl

2 tablespoons cocoa powder

2 tablespoons granulated sugar

For the paste

1 tablespoon bread flour

1 teaspoon cocoa powder

½ teaspoon fast-acting dried yeast

a pinch of salt

1 tablespoon granulated sugar

1 tablespoon vegetable oil

1 tablespoon water

salted butter, to serve

The dough itself here is very simple and perfect if all you want to do is make a basic loaf, but I always think why not add frills if you can? I, for one, like a frill, a tassel, and a fringe, so that is what this distinctive loaf is all about. The dough is laced with fragrant cinnamon and swirled with sweet cocoa. It has a distinctive look and a lovely chewy top.

Put the flour in a mixing bowl, add the cinnamon and salt on one side, and the yeast on the other. (Keeping them separate prevents the salt from killing the yeast.) Add the oil and give it all a stir. Make a well in the center and pour the water into it.

If you're using a mixer, attach a dough hook and mix till the dough forms a ball. If you don't have a mixer, bring the dough together by hand.

Now the dough needs kneading until it is smooth, stretchy, and elastic. If you are doing this by hand, lightly flour the worktop and knead for about 10 minutes. If you are using a mixer, knead with the dough hook on medium speed for 6 minutes. Then pop the dough into a lightly greased bowl, cover with greased plastic wrap, and let rise in a warm spot until doubled in size.

Once it has risen, knock the air out of the dough by punching straight into the bowl. Tip it out onto a lightly floured surface.

Have an 8½ x 4½-inch/900g loaf pan greased and ready. Roll the dough out to a 16 x 10-inch/40 x 25cm rectangle. Mix the cocoa powder and sugar in a bowl and sprinkle all over the dough.

With the shorter end closest to you, begin rolling the dough up, pulling just a little as you do so, to get the roll really tight and close. Pinch the seam together to prevent the filling from escaping. Tuck in the ends underneath, making sure the seam is on the bottom.

Drop the roll into the loaf pan, cover with greased plastic wrap, and let rise till doubled in size again.

While that happens, make the paste by mixing the flour, cocoa, yeast, salt, sugar, oil, and water together.

Preheat the oven to 425°F. As soon as the dough has doubled in size, take off the plastic wrap and gently brush the paste all over the surface of the loaf. Be generous.

Bake for 25 to 30 minutes, then take out and let cool completely in the pan. Now it's time to slice and spread with delicious cold, salted butter—the only real way to enjoy this beauty.

cherry chelsea buns

Makes 12   Prep 30 minutes, plus rising and soaking
Cook 20 minutes

For the buns

3½ cups/450g bread flour, + extra for dusting

¼ cup/50g unsalted butter, chopped

2 packages (4½ teaspoons/14g) fast-acting dried yeast

¼ cup/50g granulated sugar

1 teaspoon ground nutmeg

1 teaspoon salt

1 large egg, beaten

½ cup + 2 tablespoons/150ml warm milk

up to 5 tablespoons/75ml water

For the cherry filling

1¼ cups/200g dried cherries (or mixed berries and cherries)

1¼ cups/300ml boiling water

1 teaspoon almond extract

2 tablespoons unsalted butter, softened

2 tablespoons granulated sugar

12 glacé cherries

For the sugar glaze

½ cup/100g granulated sugar

2 tablespoons hot water

These buns are similar to those sold by that well-known Scandinavian furniture store, where I always wish they would put the cafe at the start, before the endless row of arrows, so I could grab something to sustain me throughout. Saying that, the buns do help ease the blow at the end when I've bought more than I meant to! The buns here have no cinnamon, as the dough is flavored with nutmeg instead, with a sour cherry swirl through the center, a crisp, sugary glaze, and, like all wonderful things, a cherry on top.

Pop the flour and butter in a bowl and rub in. Add the yeast, sugar, and nutmeg to one side and the salt to the other. Mix well and make a well in the center.

Mix the egg and milk in a bowl and pour into the well. With a rubber spatula, mix the ingredients to bring the dough together. If it is very dry and not coming together, add a few drops of water until it does.

Knead for 10 minutes by hand on a floured surface, or for 6 minutes on high speed using a stand mixer with a dough hook. Let rise in a warm place covered with greased plastic wrap or a damp tea towel, until doubled in size.

To make the filling, put the dried cherries in a bowl with the boiling water and let soak for at least 1 hour or until the fruits are soft, plump, and fully rehydrated. Then drain the water off and squeeze them a handful at a time to remove all moisture. Pop them into the food processor along with the almond extract, butter, and sugar and blitz to a smooth paste.

Now make the buns. Have two large baking sheets ready, lined and lightly greased. Dust the worktop with some flour. Take out the dough and roll out to form a rectangle of 10 x 18 inches/25 x 45 cm.

With the longer side closest to you, spread the filling all over, right to the edge. Roll up from the longer edge into a log. Cut into 12 equal slices and pop them onto the lined sheets, leaving lots of room around them to rise. Squash them down a little to flatten out and allow them to rise evenly. Cover with greased plastic wrap and let rise until doubled in size again.

Preheat the oven to 350°F. Pop a glacé cherry in the center of each risen bun and bake for 20 minutes, until golden and puffed up.

Meanwhile, make the glaze by mixing the sugar and hot water. Once the buns are baked and still hot, brush the glaze all over them, to get a lovely sheen.

These are perfect eaten with a hot beverage or, better still, popped in a paper bag and stuck in your pocket for any intensive shopping experience!

brioche custard buns

Makes 10
Prep 40 minutes, plus rising
Cook 35 minutes

For the brioche

3 cups/375g bread flour, + extra for dusting

1 teaspoon salt

1 package (2¼ teaspoons/7g) fast-acting dried yeast

¾ cup/175g unsalted butter, chilled

4 large eggs

whole milk, chilled

For the chocolate anise crème patissière

1 cup/240ml whole milk

3 whole star anise

4 large egg yolks

½ cup/100g granulated sugar

1 teaspoon vanilla bean paste

3 tablespoons cornstarch

¼ cup/20g cocoa powder

1 tablespoon/20g unsalted butter

To finish

1 egg, beaten, to glaze

sugar pearl nibs or sprinkles, for decoration (optional)

1 x 8-oz/220g can of peach slices

I'm a big fan of brioche and can eat it every which way, but these buns are the way I like to eat it best: sweet, soft brioche dough, filled with a chocolate custard, just kissed with the shine of star anise, and topped with a juicy slice of peach. The buns look delicate, but they are satisfyingly heavy to hold and something about this contrast makes me smile. I love a weighty sweet treat and these are that while being light and sophisticated too.

Mix the flour, salt, and yeast in a large bowl. Grate the butter straight into the flour mixture and mix well so that the separate pieces of butter get covered.

Crack the eggs into a liquid measuring cup and lightly beat till they are just broken. Now add enough milk to make up 1 cup/240ml of liquid—you might only need a splash or two. Make a well in the center of the dry ingredients, pour in the egg mixture, and mix using a rubber spatula till the dough begins to come together.

Now knead for 10 minutes on a floured surface, or, if you are using a mixer, knead with a dough hook for 6 minutes (I would highly recommend a mixer if you have one because this is quite a sticky dough). The dough should become firmer and elastic, and you should see streaks of butter all the way through.

Pop the dough back into a bowl and put in the fridge to rise for 2 hours or until doubled in size.

Now make the crème patissière by putting the milk and star anise in a pot. Pop onto high heat and bring to a rapid boil, till it's just scorched the milk, then take off the heat.

In another bowl, whisk together the egg yolks, sugar, vanilla, cornstarch, and cocoa powder till you have a really thick mixture.

Remove the star anise and slowly and gradually pour the warm milk into the egg mixture, just a small amount at a time, whisking between each addition, until it is all incorporated.

Now pop the mixture back into the milk pot and place on medium heat, whisking all the time. It should take about 3½ minutes to get a really thick chocolate crème pat.

Remove from the heat and whisk in the butter, then transfer to a bowl and cover with plastic wrap, making sure it touches the surface of the mixture to prevent it from forming a skin. Once it's cooled for 10 minutes, pop into the fridge.

When the dough has doubled in size, place on a lightly floured worktop and divide the dough into 10 equal-size dough balls. If you are being precise, each one should be 2⅔ to 2¾ oz/75 to 80g.

Have a muffin pan at the ready. On the floured worktop, roll each mound into a 4¾-inch/12cm circle, about ⅓-inch/0.75cm thick. Pop the circle of dough into a hole in the muffin pan. Push your thumb down into the dough to create a little cavity in which to place the chocolate crème pat. This will create some overhang, but that is perfect.

Do this to the other 9, then cover with a sheet of greased plastic wrap and let rise for 20 minutes.

Preheat the oven to 350°F. Scrape the cooled crème pat into a piping bag, or you can just spoon the mixture into the buns. If you need to loosen it (which you may), mix thoroughly with a spoon till it's smooth and glossy again.

Brush the edges of the brioche cups with the beaten egg and, optionally, sprinkle sugar pearl nibs (or your favorite sprinkles) all over the edges. Pipe or spoon the crème pat into each cavity, then pop a slice of peach right on top.

Bake for 25 minutes, till the edges are golden. Once baked, let them cool in the pan for 20 minutes before removing. These are equally delicious warm or cold, and perfect for breakfast, brunch, or any time of the day, really.

citrus polonaise buns

Makes 14
Prep 50 minutes, plus rising
Cook 35 minutes

For the bread

4 cups/500g bread flour, + extra for dusting

¾ cup/175g unsalted butter, very soft

1 teaspoon salt

1 package (2¼ teaspoons/7g) fast-acting dried yeast

1 lemon, finely grated zest only, saving the juice for the curd

1 orange, finely grated zest only, saving the juice for the curd

4 large eggs, lightly beaten

a few splashes of whole milk

1⅓ cups/100g mixed candied peel, chopped if large

vegetable oil, for greasing

For the citrus curd

juice of the lemon and orange as above

¾ cup/150g granulated sugar

2 tablespoons cornstarch

3 large egg yolks + 1 whole large egg (save the whites for the meringue)

7 tablespoons/100g butter, softened

For the meringue

¾ cup/150g granulated sugar

3 large egg whites (or ¾ cup/180ml if you're using egg whites out of a carton)

¼ teaspoon salt

¼ teaspoon cream of tartar

These little beauties are my take on the French classic brioche polonaise. They consist of light butter brioche laced with mixed candied peel, sliced, and filled with a citrus curd (rather than the traditional crème pat), then covered in meringue and a sprinkling of almonds and lightly toasted until golden. I admit they are not quite authentic, but I like these flavors, so I threw it all up in the air to come up with something I could call my own.

Start by making the dough. Put the flour in a large mixing bowl or the bowl of a stand mixer.

Add the butter and, using your hands, rub the butter into the flour until there are no large chunks left. Add the salt to one side of the bowl and the yeast to the other. Now add the orange and lemon zests and give everything a really good mix.

Put the eggs into a liquid measuring cup and lightly beat. Add enough milk to bring the amount of liquid up to 1 cup/240ml (you don't need to add any extra liquid if you are already at 1 cup/240ml).

Make a well in the center of the flour mixture, and pour the liquid into it. If you are doing this by hand, bring the dough together, lightly dust the surface of your worktop with flour, and knead the dough until smooth and stretchy, which will probably take about 10 minutes. If you are using a stand mixer, attach the dough hook and knead for 6 minutes on medium speed. Finally, briefly knead in the mixed candied peel. Roll the dough into a neat mound, pop into a lightly oiled bowl covered with greased plastic wrap and let rise in the fridge for 2 hours.

→

You can make the curd while you wait. Juice the lemon and orange straight into a saucepan. To the pan add the sugar, cornstarch, egg yolk, egg, and butter and whisk until thoroughly combined.

Pop the pan onto medium to low heat and whisk constantly until the mixture is really thick. This should take a few minutes. As soon as it's thick, take off the heat and transfer to a bowl. Cover it with a sheet of plastic wrap touching the surface to prevent a skin from forming and let cool.

You can use this time to make the meringue. Combine the sugar, egg whites, salt, and cream of tartar in a heatproof bowl. Set it above a pot half-full of boiling water. Make sure the bottom of the bowl doesn't touch the water, or you will have scrambled eggs.

Pop onto the heat and stir for about 3 minutes on medium heat, until the sugar has dissolved.

Now using electric beaters and with your thermometer at the ready, whisk on high speed until the temperature of the mixture is between 154 and 161°F/ 68 and 72°C. This can take up to 10 minutes.

As soon as it has reached the required temperature, take the pan off the heat and keep whisking the mixture until the bowl is just warm to the touch and the peaks are stiff. Let cool completely, cover, and place in the fridge.

Once the dough has finished rising, turn it out onto a floured work surface.

Line a baking sheet with some parchment paper.

Roll the dough to a ½-inch/1cm thickness and, using a 2¾-inch/7cm fluted cutter, cut out 14 rounds and set them on the sheet.

Cover with some greased plastic wrap and let rise for 15 minutes.

Preheat the oven to 425°F, remove the plastic wrap, and pop the sheet in. Bake for 12 to 15 minutes.

Take out of the oven and let cool completely.

Slice each one across the middle like a bun, spread with the curd, and sandwich together. If your curd has developed any lumps, just push the mixture through a fine-mesh sieve to get rid of them.

Once you have filled them all, take a bun, and spoon equal amounts of the meringue on top of each bun and use the back of a spoon to create peaks. Once coated, place it on the sheet and repeat with the rest.

Now, to finish these off, use a blowtorch to toast the tops, or pop them under a broiler—making sure to watch them carefully all of the time. These won't wait, so enjoy straightaway!

msemmen pancakes with a pistachio and mint honey

| Makes 10 | Prep 40 minutes, plus resting |
| Cook 40 minutes |

For the pancakes

3 cups/385g all-purpose flour

¼ teaspoon salt

1 teaspoon baking powder

1 tablespoon granulated sugar

1 large egg, lightly beaten

1¼ cups/300ml lukewarm water

1 quart/1 liter vegetable/sunflower oil, for greasing and cooking

⅓ cup/50g semolina, for sprinkling

For the pistachio and mint honey

⅓ cup/50g pistachios

2 tablespoons vegetable oil

1 tablespoon dried mint

12-oz/340g jar of honey

I first came across these online, when I saw a video of someone eating them. They didn't look like naan or chapati, maybe vaguely like a paratha, but they were surely a staple from somewhere and I had to know where. Eventually, I found a recipe for this wonderful Moroccan pancake-like pastry. I'm still unsure how to pronounce the name, but who cares how you say it when these delicious square pancakes are so good. I have yet to visit Morocco, but these chewy, flaky, golden treats make me want to book a flight right now.

Combine the flour, salt, baking powder, and sugar in a large bowl and mix well. Crack in the egg and mix it in, then add the water, a little at time, until it comes together to form a dough.

Lightly grease the worktop and knead the dough by hand for 5 minutes. If it starts to stick, alternate between greasing your work surface and greasing your hands. Oiling both will make for a slippy slide situation. The dough should be smooth and elastic and that's how you will know it is ready. Have a bak-ing sheet at the ready, very lightly greased. Oil is so important in this recipe.

Cover your hands in oil—be very generous—and give the dough ball a good smothering of oil too. Now take out chunks of dough and make sure they are well cov-ered in grease. If you're being precise, each ball has to be between 2 and 2⅓ oz/60 and 65g, but whatever the size you should have 10 dough balls, equal or otherwise.

Flatten each piece of dough onto the work surface then fold the edges in toward the center, bit by bit, until you have a rough ball. Turn it over so it is seam-side down, then cup your hand over the top of it and rotate it so that the dough is being rolled between your palm and the work surface to make a smooth ball. Pop on the greased sheet, pinched side down. Let rest cov-ered with a damp tea towel for 15 minutes.

Have the semolina ready in a bowl with a small spoon in it.

Grease the worktop, then take a dough ball and, using your hand, press it flat until you have a round sheet of dough, almost transparent enough to be able to see through. Be careful not to tear holes in it; it's easily done.

Sprinkle a light dusting of semolina all over, then fold the bottom third up over the middle third of the dough. Sprinkle with more semolina. Bring the top third down over the folded dough and sprinkle with semolina again. What you should have created is a long rectangle, made up of three layers of pastry.

Working from the short end, from left to right fold one third of the dough over the middle third. Sprinkle with semolina. Then, from right to left, fold the remaining third over the top. What you should be left with now is a square. If not, don't panic, it will still be delicious. Pop it back onto the sheet and do the same with the rest, until you have completed them all.

Lay the tea towel back on top and let rest for 15 minutes.

Meanwhile, make the pistachio and mint honey by putting the pistachios in a food processor with the oil and blitzing till you have a smooth paste. Then add the mint and honey and whiz until it all comes together. Pop back into the jar (or your serving dish) and set aside. This should keep for up to 1 month stored in a jar, but it won't last, because you will finish it with these flaky, chewy beauties. I promise.

Now to make the msemmen: grease the worktop lightly (I told you there was a fair amount of greasing involved in this recipe), pop one square down and, using a rolling pin, roll till the square is at least three times the size, about 6 x 6 inches/15 x 15cm. Repeat with all of them and pile them back on the sheet. They are oiled enough to not stick to one another, don't worry.

To cook, pop a small glug of oil into a nonstick frying pan on medium to high heat. All our stovetops are different so you will get a feel for what is right once you cook the first one.

Add the msemmen and cook for 3 minutes on one side, then flip over and cook for 1 minute on the other. They should puff up slightly while cooking and have dots of golden brown all over.

Repeat with all the msemmen and keep them wrapped in the tea towel to keep them soft and warm.

To eat, smother with the pistachio and mint honey and roll. They are best served with a hot steaming cup of mint tea.

honeycomb rolls

Makes 13
Prep 35 minutes, plus rising
Cook 25 minutes

For the honeycomb

1 cup/200g granulated sugar

3 tablespoons/60g golden syrup or light corn syrup

2 teaspoons baking soda

For the bread rolls

7 tablespoons/100g plain yogurt

3¼ cups/400g all-purpose flour, + extra for dusting

2 tablespoons granulated sugar

¼ teaspoon salt

1 package (2¼ teaspoons/7g) fast-acting dried yeast

¾ cup + 2 tablespoons/ 200ml lukewarm water

vegetable oil, for greasing

For the honeycomb filling

½ cup + 1 tablespoon/ 125g mascarpone

⅓ cup/50g white sesame seeds

2 tablespoons tahini

For the topping

1 tablespoon butter, melted

1 teaspoon white or black sesame seeds

These are traditionally known as honeycomb rolls because of the way they are arranged: sweet little buns misaligned by one, to create a honeycomb effect. But with such a great name, I couldn't resist incorporating actual honeycomb somehow. So I've filled them with mascarpone sweetened with a bittersweet honeycomb dust and a hint of tahini for nuttiness, then covered in more of that delicious honeycomb and finally dusted with sesame seeds. If you don't want to make the honeycomb yourself, you could use that famous chocolate bar with its perfectly thin chocolate edge, but I think you should give the homemade stuff a try, especially if you never have before, because you'll find it's surprisingly easy.

To make the honeycomb, put the sugar in a large pot along with the golden syrup. This magical stuff expands really quickly, so you do need a decent-size pot. Have a baking sheet lined and greased, ready for the honeycomb to be poured onto. Prep is key here—molten sugar allows no dilly-dallying! Have your baking soda ready measured beside you along with your whisk and a heatproof spatula.

Pop the pot onto medium to high heat. Stay close, and be ready to lower the heat or even take the pot off the heat if need be.

Stir the sugar and syrup to gently combine. It should begin to sizzle and the sugar should start to melt. Don't mix the whole time, just occasionally. You will see the sugar around the outside start to go darker first—that's when you should give it a little stir and encourage the darker sugar to mix with the lighter.

→

Take off the heat as soon as the mixture is an even deep-amber color (if you have a sugar thermometer, the temperature should have reached 302°F/150°C). This should take somewhere between 3 and 4 minutes.

Tip the baking soda in and use your whisk to whisk it in fast—no time to wait here. Honeycomb waits for no man! It should start to really puff up and take over your pan like some 1980s horror movie goopy ghoul! Take the whisk out once all the baking soda

has been incorporated and use the spatula to pour and scrape it all out into the lined baking sheet and allow it to expand by itself. Let it cool for at least 2 hours while you get on with the rest of the recipe. Don't be tempted to touch it—your fingertips will thank me later!

Meanwhile, make the bread dough by adding the yogurt to the flour in a bowl and use a rubber spatula to roughly combine them. Now add the sugar and salt to the bowl on one side and the yeast to the other side. (This is to prevent the salt from killing the yeast.) Give it another good mix. Make a well in the center and add the water. Use the same spatula to bring the dough together.

Generously dust the work surface with flour, and bring the dough together on it until it is no longer too sticky. Knead for 5 minutes.

After 5 minutes, grease the work surface with oil and knead again for another 5 minutes. The dough should be smooth and a little more elastic. Put it into a greased bowl, cover with a damp tea towel, and let rise until doubled in size.

Meanwhile, to make the filling, measure out 1¾ oz/ 50g of the honeycomb and roughly crush it. Combine it with the mascarpone, sesame seeds, and tahini.

Line a small baking sheet with some parchment paper and lightly grease.

Knock the air out of the dough and tip it onto a flour-dusted work surface.

Tear mounds off the dough until you have 13 equal pieces (1¾ to 2 oz/50 to 55g each). Using the palm of your hand, squash down until you have a flat round piece of dough ready to be filled. Do this to all of them.

Take the filling mixture and add a heaped spoonful to each bit of dough, making sure to divide it evenly, until you have used up all the mixture.

Take a circle of dough, pick it up, and bring the edges into the center to enclose the filling, pinching as you go. Be sure to give it a really good pinch so that the filling doesn't ooze out. It still might even after your efforts, but that's OK. Repeat with all the dough.

Pop them pinched-side down on the sheet, leaving just a small gap to allow the buns to expand while rising, and arrange them in honeycomb style.

Cover with a damp tea towel or greased plastic wrap and let rise for 30 minutes.

Preheat the oven to 400°F and bake the rolls in the oven for 15 minutes, until they are wonderfully golden.

Meanwhile, melt the butter. Measure another 1¾ oz/ 50g of honeycomb and roughly crush it. When the rolls are baked, get the sheet straight out onto a cooling rack and brush them immediately with the hot melted butter, then be generous with the honeycomb and sesame seeds. Doing this while they are still hot is essential for the honeycomb to melt and stick to the buns.

Let cool for at least 30 minutes before eating. I love to have these with a steaming-hot cup of tea, but it has to be strongly brewed alongside something as sweet and gooey as this. The remaining unused honeycomb can be kept in an airtight container.

salmon and dill stuffed focaccia

Makes 1 large sheet / **Serves** 8 as a side
Prep 30 minutes, plus rising   **Cook** 30 minutes

Focaccia is by far one of my favorite breads. Although it's easy to buy, it's also easy to make and the texture of freshly baked focaccia is like nothing else. The chewy, airy bread is just the best, but made better with every bite when you get a flood of really good oil. In this case I am using clarified butter, because it has a flavor like no other, and infused with the garlic it's just out of this world. This focaccia is so much more than just a layer of bread, too, because before baking it is filled with delicious smoked salmon and dill.

For the dough

4 cups/500g bread flour, + more for dusting

2 tablespoons clarified butter

2 teaspoons salt

2 packages (4½ teaspoons/14g) fast-acting dried yeast

1½ cups/350ml lukewarm water, + more as needed

vegetable oil, for greasing the bowl and baking sheet

semolina, for dusting

For drizzling

7 tablespoons/100g clarified butter

2 cloves of garlic, peeled and thinly sliced

For the filling

3½ oz/100g smoked salmon

a small handful of fresh dill, finely chopped

1 teaspoon ground black pepper

a sprinkle of sea salt flakes

Put the flour into a large mixing bowl, add the butter, and quickly rub it in with your hands until it has disappeared totally into small crumbs. Now add the salt on one side of the bowl and the yeast on the other. Give it all a quick mix, then make a well in the center and add all the liquid, then use a rubber spatula to bring the dough together as much as possible. If the dough is too floury to come together, mix in up to 2 tablespoons more water.

A mixer with a dough hook is best for kneading this, as the dough can be a little sticky and I hate it when most of it ends up on my hands. If you are kneading by hand, make sure to lightly dust both the work surface and your hands with flour at the start and again whenever it feels too sticky. Whatever method you choose, knead the dough for 10 minutes until smooth, stretchy, and elastic. Keep adding small amounts of flour if it keeps sticking, but not too much. Put it in a lightly greased bowl, cover with greased plastic wrap or a damp tea towel, and let rise until doubled in size. The time can vary depending on the warmth of the place you put it; you will find the perfect spot for rising the more you bake.

While that is happening, get the clarified butter for the drizzle into a pan over high heat. As soon as it starts to smoke, add the sliced garlic, then remove the pan from the heat. The butter should be hot enough to really brown that garlic, so now set it aside to infuse and allow the butter to cool.

Prepare a rimmed baking sheet with a light layer of oil and sprinkling of semolina. Tip the dough out onto the sheet, generously oil your hands to prevent it from sticking to you, then encourage and spread the dough out into an 8 x 12-inch/20 x 30cm rectangle.

Cover one half of the rectangle with the smoked salmon, and sprinkle on the dill and the ground black pepper. Take the other half of the dough and fold it over to encase that lovely filling. Turn the dough so it fits comfortably in the center of the sheet. Using your hands, again push that dough all the way out into an 8 x 12-inch/20 x 30cm rectangle. Now, cover with some greased plastic wrap or a damp tea towel and let rise until doubled in size again.

Preheat the oven to 425°F.

Use your fingers to poke dents all over the dough. It may feel a little weird, but it also feels a little good! Don't press all the way through the dough, but just enough to create great big indents where your garlicky clarified butter will pool.

Once you have done that, drizzle with the melted butter, reserving the garlic slices to use later. Make sure the butter fills all those dents. It may look like an awful lot, but don't worry; the dough wants it and will absorb it all, making for the most delicious focaccia, I promise, so go for it.

Bake for 20 to 25 minutes, until golden brown.

Take the focaccia out, give it a good sprinkling of salt, and scatter the browned garlic slices over the top.

Let cool before eating, as this will encourage the oils to absorb right back in.

This is perfect as a side for a main dish, but I really enjoy this on a picnic, because it's a delicious chewy bread with a delicious filling all set to go.

rose harissa rugelach

Makes 12 (harissa makes about 2 cups/520g and will keep in fridge up to 2 weeks or freezer up to 3 months)   **Prep** 40 minutes, plus resting   **Cook** 45 minutes

My favorite episode of *The Apprentice* is when the contestants have to drive all around town to find obscure items. One year they had to find rugelach, and before anyone even failed that challenge I was off researching these little beauties. A Polish, bready, but almost short bake that is layered with chocolate and then rolled up to look like little croissants—they're delicious yet dangerous, because I can eat about ten in one sitting. For this recipe, however, I have replaced the chocolate with homemade rose harissa. The flavor is spicy yet sweet, with the fiercest of reds twirled in that short, creamy pastry. You can easily replace the harissa with more traditional flavors, but this is one worth trying.

For the harissa

5 tablespoons coriander seeds (about 30g)

5 tablespoons cumin seeds (about 40g)

5 tablespoons fennel seeds (about 40g)

5 tablespoons chile flakes (about 30g)

10 organic roses, petals pulled apart

2 whole heads of garlic, peeled

1 medium red onion, peeled and chopped

1 large red bell pepper, seeded and chopped

1 tablespoon salt

7 tablespoons/100ml olive oil, + extra if needed

For the rugelach

¼ cup/160g all-purpose flour, + extra for dusting

1¾ teaspoons baking powder

¼ teaspoon salt

½ cup/120g chilled butter, roughly cubed

4½ oz/120g full-fat cream cheese, chilled

butter or oil, for greasing the baking sheet

1 egg, beaten, for glazing

cracked black pepper

→

For the harissa, combine the coriander, cumin, and fennel seeds in a nonstick pan and toast on high heat until they begin to pop.

Transfer the toasted seeds to a blender and add all the other harissa ingredients, except the oil. Whiz everything together to a smooth paste. If you find the mixture too stiff, add a few spoons of extra oil to help it along.

Pour the oil into a pan, add the paste, and cook on low heat for 15 minutes, until it is dry, rich, and thick. Transfer to a jar and set aside to cool completely.

Now for the rugelach. Put the flour, baking powder, and salt into a food processor. Add the butter and whiz until you have large buttery clumps. Next, add the cream cheese and whiz until the mixture comes together into a large ball. Wrap and chill for 1 hour to firm up the dough. Prepare a baking sheet by lining it with some lightly greased parchment paper.

Tip the dough, which can be quite sticky, out onto a generously floured surface. Roll it into a rectangle about 14 x 10 inches/35 x 25 cm. Take 2 heaped tablespoons of the harissa and spread it all over the pastry. With the longest side facing you, cut the rectangle into 6 equal vertical strips. Then cut each strip on the diagonal, starting at the bottom and going all the way up to the opposite corner to create a triangle. Do this to each strip, which will give you 12 triangles in total.

Taking one triangle at a time, and with the widest part of it closest to you, roll gently toward the point—you should end up with what look like sweet little croissants. Place on the sheet with the little point of the triangle underneath, so it doesn't just pop up. Repeat this with all the triangles. Place them a little distance apart, but these don't spread or grow much so don't be worried if you have a smaller sheet. Put into the fridge to chill for 30 minutes.

Preheat the oven to 350°F.

Take the sheet out of the fridge, brush the rugelach all over with some beaten egg, and dust with a little cracked black pepper. Bake in the oven for 25 to 30 minutes, until they are light, crisp, and golden brown among the fiery red.

Let cool completely before eating, or at least try!

pulled chicken doughnuts

Makes 12 **Prep** 35 minutes, plus rising and chilling
Cook 40 minutes

For the bread

4⅓ cups/550g bread flour, + extra for dusting

¾ cup/175g unsalted butter, softened

¼ cup/60g granulated sugar

1 teaspoon salt

2 packages (4½ teaspoons/14g) fast-acting dried yeast

4 large eggs, lightly beaten

7 tablespoons/100ml cold water

1½ quarts/1½ liters vegetable oil, to deep fry

For the chicken filling

1 large chicken breast or 2 small—around 10oz/280g

7 tablespoons/100ml barbecue sauce

3 tablespoons mayonnaise

1 teaspoon chile flakes

1 small handful of fresh chives, finely chopped

For the savory dust

1 teaspoon granulated garlic

1 teaspoon ground cumin

1 teaspoon salt

1 teaspoon granulated sugar

1 teaspoon dried cilantro

Doughnuts filled with chicken, need I say more? But seeing as you're here and I have your attention, I will. These doughnuts are filled with a quick-cooked shredded chicken, then fried and covered in a delicious savory-sweet dust. If anyone didn't know these were savory, they could be fooled. This recipe is worth a try just to see the confusion and delight on people's faces.

Start by making the dough. Put the flour in a bowl, add the butter, and rub in until there are no big butter chunks remaining. Now add the sugar and salt to one side of the bowl and the yeast to the other side. Mix thoroughly and then make a well in the center. Mix the eggs and water in a bowl, then pour into the well and mix with the dry ingredients until the dough roughly comes together.

If you are kneading the dough by hand, flour the work surface and knead for 10 minutes, until the dough is stretchy and shiny. But I prefer to do it using a mixer, as the dough is quite sticky and buttery. When using a dough hook on a mixer it only needs kneading for 6 minutes on medium speed.

Let rise in a warm place, covered with a damp tea towel or greased plastic wrap.

Meanwhile, make the filling by boiling the chicken breast in a small pot of water on medium heat for 15 minutes, until the meat is cooked through.

Once cooked, lift the chicken out of the water and set aside in a bowl until it's cool enough to handle. Use two forks to shred and pull it apart. Now add flavor to your chicken by adding the barbecue sauce, mayo, chile flakes, and chives and giving it all a good mix around. Cover and set aside in the fridge.

Once the dough has doubled in size, tip out onto a floured work surface. Roll the dough into a sausage shape and cut out 12 equal portions of around 3¼ oz/90g each. Making them the same size is important if you want them to fry evenly.

Have a lined and greased baking sheet at the ready. Roll out a dough ball to 4¾ inch/12cm in diameter.

→

Add a tablespoon of chicken mix, not heaped, into the center. Gently lift up the edges of the dough from all around the sides and seal the chicken inside, pinching firmly in the center. Pop it on the sheet, pinched side up.

Do this to the rest of the dough balls, then pop the sheet into the fridge for 1 hour.

In the meantime, make the dust by mixing the garlic, cumin, salt, sugar, and cilantro.

Just before the hour is up, pour the oil into a medium pot. Make sure the oil is not higher than halfway up the sides. Heat the oil on medium heat—if you are using a thermometer you want the oil to reach 302°F/150°C. But if not, you can drop a piece of bread into the oil and if it sizzles and rises to the top, the oil is ready.

Preheat the oven to 350°F. Prepare a baking sheet lined with paper towels to drain the doughnuts on.

Gently place a doughnut into the oil, pinched side up. Don't overcrowd the pan; just do three at a time.

Cook the doughnuts gently for 6 minutes until golden brown all over. You don't need to turn them, just occasionally push them down into the oil using a slotted spoon. When ready, take out and pop onto the paper to drain, then pop in the oven for 10 minutes to finish cooking through, removing the paper towels first. While still piping hot, sprinkle with the savory dust. Do the same to all of them, frying and sprinkling.

Allow to cool down, then eat them lukewarm, or even totally cooled. All I can say is: you are welcome!

cheat's sourdough

This ingredients list is in two parts, as the making of this spans over 24 hours. I mean, there is being ready with everything weighed out, but so far in advance would be too much to ask.

> **Makes** 1 large loaf
> **Prep** 30 minutes, plus rising
> **Cook** 30 minutes

1st set of ingredients

1½ cups/200g bread flour

¾ cup + 2 tablespoons/ 200ml water

1 package (2¼ teaspoons/7g) fast-acting dried yeast

2nd set of ingredients

3 cups + 2 tablespoons/ 400g bread flour

¾ cup + 2 tablespoons/ 200ml water

1 package (2¼ teaspoons/7g) fast-acting dried yeast

1 teaspoon salt

Many a sourdough starter has come and gone in my house, but none has remained long enough for me to hand it down to anyone! With eighteen tropical fish, four laying hens, a budgie named Rayf, and a rabbit named Cornelius, when we go away my neighbors have their hands full enough in keeping our little zoo alive, so I can hardly ask them to also tend to my sourdough (which is always named Julio: Julio the Sourdough!). So this is my cheat's version. The dough sours overnight and is ready after 24 hours.

Decide when you want to eat your fresh bread. I tend to begin the recipe between 6 and 7 a.m. on a Saturday, so I can knead, rise, bake, and eat 24 hours later.

I like to start by using the bowl that I will later knead my dough in, which for me is always the bowl of my stand mixer. Or simply use a large bowl. Combine the first set of ingredients (flour, water, yeast) in the bowl and give the gloopy liquid a really good mix. Cover with a damp tea towel and let rise in a warm spot for 24 hours to bubble away and sour gently.

Now it's time for the second set of ingredients, so add the flour, water, yeast, and salt to the bubbling dough.

Attach a dough hook to your mixer and mix on low speed until the dough comes together. When it forms a ball, turn the mixer up and knead on medium speed for about 6 minutes. If you are doing it by hand, knead on a floured surface for 10 minutes, until it's smooth, stretchy, and elastic.

It's best to let this rise in the pot you will bake it in. Find a large, 5-quart/5-liter cast-iron pot with a lid (or a normal saucepan, but make sure it doesn't have a plastic handle, as it needs to go in the oven), and line with a large piece of parchment paper, pushing it to the bottom and around the sides. Tuck the edges of the dough under itself so you have a nice round, smooth mound. Pop into the pot, cover with the lid, and let rise for about 30 minutes or until it has doubled in size.

Preheat the oven to 425°F. As soon as the dough is ready, cut a few slashes in the top and pop the pot into the oven with the lid on. Bake for 30 to 40 minutes, until light golden on top and slightly darker around the edges. Letting it bake this way traps the steam, which creates a nice crust.

Once the pot is out of the oven, take off the lid and allow the loaf to cool completely in the pot. Then take out, slice, and eat—your way! I like butter and salt, then I move on to butter and jam, then butter and cheese, and then I repeat, till there is no bread left.

mashed potato flatbreads with egg butter

Makes 6   **Prep** 30 minutes   **Cook** 20 minutes

For the flatbreads

1⅔ cups/400g cooled mashed potato (use leftovers, buy pre-made, or even use instant mash!)

1 large egg, lightly beaten

1¼ cups/150g all-purpose flour

½ teaspoon salt

2 teaspoons cumin seeds

vegetable oil, for greasing

For the egg butter

3 large eggs, boiled and cooled

½ cup + 1 tablespoon/125g unsalted butter, softened

½ teaspoon onion salt (or normal salt if you can't find any)

1 teaspoon ground black pepper

2 teaspoons dried parsley

These are a great alternative to flour flatbreads. They are soft, delicious, and very simple. Perfect for when you have leftover mashed potatoes you need to use up, or when you want to try something different. They are subtly spiced with delicious cumin seeds and topped off with a butter that has been mixed with eggs—the butter melts and leaves behind that wonderful, rich, crumbled egg.

Start by making the flatbread dough. Put the mashed potato in a bowl, add the egg, and mix together. Add the flour, salt, and cumin seeds and mix it all in really well until you have a dough that feels more difficult to mix as it stiffens.

Preheat the oven to 425°F. Line two baking sheets with parchment paper and lightly grease.

Generously oil your hands and divide the dough into 6 equal pieces. If you want to be precise, each one should be around 3½ oz/100g.

Still with very greased hands, roll the dough mounds into balls. The mixture is still quite soft, so take your time. Pop three onto each sheet and, using the palm of your hand, press into circles with a diameter of roughly 4¾ inches/12cm. Prick all over the surface of the circles to prevent them from puffing up.

Bake for 18 to 20 minutes. They are ready when the outsides are golden but the centers are still soft.

Meanwhile, make the egg butter by combining the boiled eggs, butter, onion salt, pepper, and parsley in a food processor and blitzing until you have a smooth, eggy mixture.

Take the flatbreads out of the oven and wrap in a clean tea towel to keep them warm and soft.

When you are ready to serve, spread with copious amounts of the egg butter. Any leftover egg butter will keep in the fridge for up to 3 days.

onion pretzels

4 cups/500g bread flour, + extra for dusting

1 package (2¼ teaspoons /7g) fast-acting dried yeast

2 tablespoons granulated sugar

⅓ cup/30g crispy fried onions

1 tablespoon granulated onion

2 teaspoons dried chives

¼ cup/50g unsalted butter, melted, + extra for greasing the baking sheets

1¼ cups/300ml warm water

3 tablespoons baking soda

To finish

1 large egg, lightly beaten

1 teaspoon paprika

1 teaspoon granulated onion

1 teaspoon salt

Makes 12   Prep 45 minutes, plus rising
Cook 25 minutes

Pretzels are surprisingly easy to make and these ones are even easier because, instead of the usual intricate shape, I just do knots. Laced with crispy onions and chives and then topped with a dusting of intense onion flavor, they are soft and yummy and super satisfying.

Start by putting the flour in a large mixing bowl with the yeast, sugar, fried onions, granulated onion, and chives and mix until well combined.

Add the butter and mix well using your fingertips or a pastry cutter. Make a well in the center. Add the water and mix until the dough comes together.

Attach the dough hook to a stand mixer and knead for 5 minutes on medium speed, until the dough is smooth and stretchy. Cover and let rise until doubled in size.

Grease two baking sheets. Take the dough out and divide into 12 equal-size balls, about 2½ oz/75g each. Roll out each ball to a 12-inch/30cm sausage shape and then tie into a knot (see photo on the next page), tuck the ends underneath, and pop onto the greased sheets. Let rise covered with greased plastic wrap for just 15 minutes.

Preheat the oven to 400°F.

Bring a large saucepan of water to a boil. Add the baking soda, stir in well until dissolved, then let simmer. Gently drop in a few of the dough knots (just enough so they don't touch) and cook for 10 seconds. Flip with a slotted spoon and cook for another 10 seconds.

Drain and pop back onto the greased sheet. Repeat with the rest. Glaze them with the beaten egg. Mix the paprika, granulated onion, and salt together, sprinkle all over the knots, and bake for 12 minutes. Take out, let cool a little on a rack, and eat while they are still warm.

→

→

cardamom lemon iced buns

Makes 12 **Prep** 25 minutes **Cook** 15 minutes

The first time I tried classic iced buns was when I found them on sale at the supermarket with a yellow sticker calling to me! At about 15 cents a pack, how could I not? The bag was slightly torn, the bread was slightly stale, but those things aside, I thought their sweet icing and fragrant nutmeg-kissed flavor was simply delicious. Here I have created my own version with a few little differences. These are fragrant with cardamom and lemon zest, while the juice of the lemon is used to make a super-sweet and equally tart icing.

For the buns

4 cups/500g bread flour, + extra for dusting

2 packages (4½ teaspoons/14g) fast-acting dried yeast

¼ cup/50g granulated sugar

2 teaspoons salt

¼ cup/60ml sunflower oil, + extra for greasing

7 cardamom pods, seeds removed and crushed, or 2 teaspoons ground cardamom

finely grated zest of 2 lemons

2 large eggs, lightly beaten

½ cup + 2 tablespoons/ 150ml warm water

½ cup + 2 tablespoons/ 150ml warm milk

For the icing

3¼ cups/400g confectioners' sugar

5 tablespoons/75ml lemon juice, from the zested lemons

Start with the dough. Put the flour in a large mixing bowl. Add the yeast and sugar to one side of the bowl and the salt to the other side. Add the oil, cardamom, and lemon zest and give it all a mix.

In another bowl, mix together the eggs, water, and milk. Make a well in the center of the dry ingredients and pour in the liquid.

Now it's time to knead. This is a wet, sticky dough, so I highly recommend using a stand mixer or hand mixer with a dough hook, on medium speed. By hand it will take longer and you'll need to flour the work surface and your hands as you go along.

Knead until the dough is smooth, shiny, and very elastic, then place in a lightly greased bowl, cover with greased plastic wrap or a damp tea towel, and let rise in a warm place until doubled in size. As it rises you should be able to smell the cardamom.

Once the dough has doubled in size, tip it out onto a floured surface. Knock out all the air.

Have a greased baking sheet at the ready. Divide the dough into 12 mounds. Each 2½ to 3 oz/75 to 80g, if you're being precise. Roll each one into a sausage shape about 4 inches/10cm long. Place them on the sheet with gaps of about ¾ inch/2cm between each one. Pop a greased piece of plastic wrap on top and let rise again until they have doubled in size. As

this happens, they will just touch and then can be baked in a batch.

Preheat the oven to 400°F. Once the buns have risen, bake in the oven for 10 to 15 minutes, then let cool on the sheet.

Make the icing by mixing the confectioners' sugar and lemon juice together to a smooth paste. Once the buns have cooled completely (this is important, or the icing will just run off), tear off a bun and dip the top side in the icing until it is covered, scraping off the excess. Do the same to the rest.

These are best eaten as soon as you can, while the bread is still really soft and fresh.

chapter eight

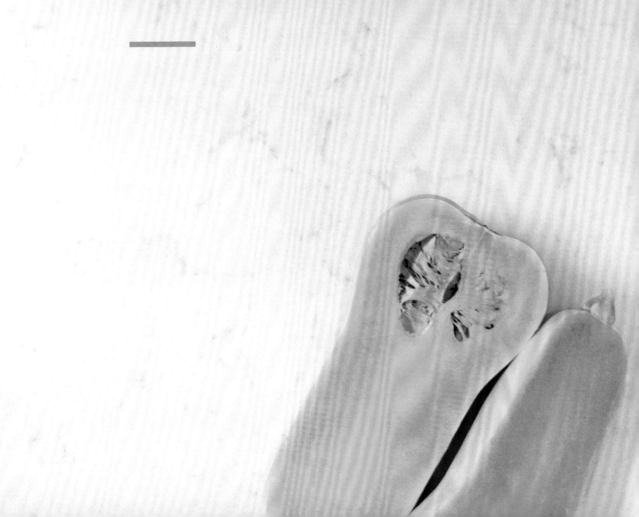

SAVORY BAKES

seekh kebab toad in the hole

For the seekh kebab

1 pound 2 oz/500g ground lamb or beef

1 small red onion, very finely diced

a small handful of cilantro, chopped

2 tablespoons garam masala

1 tablespoon chickpea flour or cornstarch

1 teaspoon salt

1 large egg

For the roasting dish

6 tablespoons/90g ghee or clarified butter

1 tablespoon coriander seeds, crushed

2 medium red onions, quartered

1 medium red bell pepper, cored and cut into 8 chunks

2 tomatoes, quartered

For the batter

1 cup + 2 tablespoons/ 140g all-purpose flour

½ teaspoon salt

2 large eggs

¾ cup/175ml whole milk

Serves 4   Prep 30 minutes, plus chilling
Cook 50 minutes

This is toad in the hole, Asian style! I'm a big fan of the original, but I like to mix things up and do what I call "desi style," so instead of sausages this contains meatballs that are spiced gently and cooked with chunks of onions, then enveloped in a Yorkshire pudding-type batter.

Start by making the seekh kebab mixture. Put the ground meat in a bowl with the onion, cilantro, garam masala, chickpea flour, salt, and egg, then get your hands in and mix the whole lot together until you have an even mixture. Divide into 12 equal mounds. Using wet hands, create small even neat rounds, pop them onto a plate, and let chill in the fridge while you prep the rest of the recipe.

Preheat the oven to 425°F. Put the ghee into an ovenproof roasting dish (about 12 inches/30cm in diameter) and pop into the oven to melt. This should only take 5 minutes.

Drop in the coriander seeds, onion, red bell pepper, and tomatoes, mix well, then return to the oven to cook for 10 minutes. The perfect time to make your batter.

Put the flour in a bowl with the salt and mix. Make a well in the center, add the eggs and milk, then, using a whisk, bring the thick batter together.

Take the roasting dish out of the oven and carefully place the kebabs in it. Put back into the oven for 10 minutes—just enough to seal the meat.

Take the roasting dish out again and gently reposition everything so there are 3 kebabs per portion and all the veg are nicely placed, before pouring in the batter.

Bake for 30 to 35 minutes. The batter will puff up and envelop the kebabs as it cooks. Let cool for 10 minutes before serving.

baked chile churros

For the churros

1⅔ cups/400ml water

¾ cup + 2 tablespoons/ 200g unsalted butter, roughly chopped

1½ cups/200g bread flour, sifted

2 teaspoons paprika

approx. 2 teaspoons chile flakes, depending on how spicy you like it

4 large eggs, lightly beaten, + 1 lightly beaten egg for brushing

3½ oz/100g mature Cheddar cheese, finely grated

2 teaspoons onion salt

2 teaspoons dried chives

For the tomato dip

9 small tomatoes (about 1 pound 5 oz/600g)

3 tablespoons olive oil

1½ teaspoons black sesame seeds

¾ teaspoon onion salt

¾ teaspoon granulated sugar

1 large clove of garlic, crushed

Makes approx. 40–45   **Prep** 40 minutes
Cook 20 minutes   **Best eaten** fresh
(but sauce can be made up to 24 hours ahead)

Can I still call these churros if they are baked instead of deep-fried, and savory instead of sweet? I think so. Whatever they are, they're delicious.

Begin by making the dough for the churros. Put the water in a medium nonstick saucepan along with the butter and pop onto high heat. Bring to a boil and as soon as the butter has melted, remove from the heat.

Now combine the flour, paprika, and chile in a bowl and mix thoroughly.

Quickly tip the flour mixture into the water/butter mixture and beat vigorously until you have a smooth, even paste. Pop the pot back onto low heat and continue to mix until you have a dough that is just coming away from the sides.

Take off the heat and give it a vigorous stir to cool it down, which should take about 2 minutes.

Add the 4 lightly beaten eggs, a little at a time, making sure to stir well between additions. It might look lumpy and separated, but will come together as you keep mixing, so persevere.

Keep adding until all the eggs are used up.

Now pop the dough into a separate bowl to cool completely. Once it has, add the grated cheese and mix well, then put it in a piping bag. I like to use a large star-tip nozzle, because it creates texture that gets crunchy in the oven, but you could also use a plain one. Preheat the oven to 425°F and prepare three baking sheets lined with some parchment paper.

Pipe lines on the sheets, approx. 2¾ inches/7cm long, leaving a gap of ½ inch/1cm in between to give them room to expand.

→

Do this until you have piped all the mixture, then brush gently with the beaten egg and sprinkle with the onion salt and dried chives.

Pop the sheets into the oven and bake for 23 to 25 minutes, making sure to move them around half-way through so everything bakes evenly.

Meanwhile, you can get on with making the tomato dip, which couldn't be simpler. Pierce each tomato with the tip of a knife—this will make them easier to peel later. Put the tomatoes in a small pot with enough water to fully submerge them. Pop onto high heat and boil for 1 to 2 minutes.

Take off the heat, drain, and as soon as they are cool enough to handle, gently remove the skins.

Chop them up, seeds and all, and set aside.

Pour the oil into a small saucepan. As soon as it is hot, add the black sesame seeds. When they pop, add the onion salt, sugar, and garlic, cook for a few seconds, and then drop in the chopped tomatoes and cook on low heat until any excess liquid has evaporated and the mixture has thickened up—this can take about 5 minutes.

Put into a serving dish.

Take the churros out of the oven and let them cool on the sheet for 20 minutes before moving them, then transfer to a serving dish and they are ready to eat with the tomato dip.

saag paneer spanakopita

For the filling

1 pound 10 oz/750g spinach

¼ cup/60g ghee or clarified butter or unsalted butter, + extra for greasing

1–4 teaspoons chile flakes, depending on how hot you like it

1½ tablespoons/8g cumin seeds

8oz/225g paneer, grated

6 cloves of garlic, crushed

2 small onions, finely diced

1½ teaspoons salt

6 tablespoons/100g ricotta

1 large egg, lightly beaten

a handful of cilantro, chopped

a handful of chives, chopped

For the pastry crust

9½ oz/270g filo pastry, defrosted if frozen

7 tablespoons/100g ghee or clarified butter or unsalted butter, melted, for brushing

2 tablespoons sesame seeds

> **Serves** 4   **Prep** 30 minutes
> **Cook** 50 minutes

Saag paneer (a dish of spinach and paneer cheese) is one of my favorite things to eat. It's not a dish I grew up with, as cheese doesn't feature often—if ever—in Bangladeshi cuisine, but as our family expanded and mixed and my palate became ever more adventurous, it's something I loved to order when we ate out, especially if it wasn't a halal eatery, as paneer was always a good, textured alternative to meat. This recipe fuses it with a spanakopita, the classic Greek filo pastry pie. Thanks to the pastry, no chapatis are required; it's an all-in-one kind of situation.

Start by making the filling. Put the spinach in a large bowl, pour boiling water all over it, and use a spoon to dunk all the leaves under the surface. Let wilt for 5 minutes.

Drain and rinse under cold water and, as soon as it is cool enough to handle, squeeze out as much moisture as you physically can. Chop then finely slice the clumps of spinach, before setting aside.

Now add the ghee to a nonstick frying pan. As soon as it is hot, add the chile flakes and cumin seeds and heat gently until the seeds begin to pop. Add the paneer and cook for 5 minutes, until you start to get some golden color on it. Add the garlic and onions and cook for 5 minutes, until the onions are soft.

Add the salt and spinach and cook until there is no moisture at all left at the bottom of the pan.

Take off the heat and let cool totally. Then add the ricotta, egg, cilantro, and chives and mix well.

Preheat the oven to 375°F. Grease the inside of an 8-inch/20cm square baking pan.

Brush a sheet of filo all over with ghee and pop it into the center of the greased pan, leaving overhang on two sides.

Get another sheet, brush it with ghee, then pop it into the pan as before, making sure that this time the overhang is on the other two sides.

Do the same with another sheet, but this time place it in the pan at an angle, and do the same with another sheet, adding that on the opposite angle.

What you should have now is the pan lined with filo, and with overhang on all the sides. Grease your three remaining sheets of filo and set them aside while you put the cooked filling into the pan and flatten the top.

Fold the overhanging pastry edges up and over the top, ruffling them gently as you do. Now take each of the extra sheets, crumple them up, and place them gently on top until the filling is entirely covered. Sprinkle with the sesame seeds.

Put into the oven and bake for 30 to 35 minutes, until the filling is hot and the pastry is crisp and golden. Let cool for 15 minutes before eating.

pepperoni pull-apart

Serves 6
Prep 30 minutes, plus resting
Cook 25 minutes

For the dough

3¼ cups/400g all-purpose flour, + extra for dusting

4¾ teaspoons baking powder

1 tablespoon dried oregano

1 tablespoon granulated sugar

1¾ teaspoons salt

1 package (2¼ teaspoons/7g) fast-acting dried yeast

1¼ cups/300ml warm water

For the filling

3 tablespoons olive oil for brushing, + extra for greasing the pan

¼ cup/60ml sriracha sauce (or chile/tomato sauce of your choice)

8 cheese slices of your choice

3 oz/80g thinly sliced pepperoni, about 16 slices

8 basil leaves

With all the flavors of a pizza, this is perfect for when you want more than just a regular slice of bread with your soup. It's very simple to create, but looks and tastes like you have made a real effort. Best of all, it's great for sharing, which is exactly the kind of food I love to eat.

Begin by making the dough. Combine the flour, baking powder, oregano, sugar, salt, and yeast in a large bowl, or the bowl of a stand mixer, making sure to keep the salt and yeast on separate sides until you begin. Then mix everything together.

Make a well in the center, add the water, and mix the dough until it starts to come together.

Now either flour a work surface and knead the dough by hand, or attach a dough hook and knead in the stand mixer. If you are doing it by hand it should take 10 to 12 minutes of continual kneading. If you are doing it by machine, 6 minutes on medium speed should do the trick.

What you are looking for is a stretchy dough that is smooth, shiny, and still just a little bit tacky.

Once it is ready, cover the bowl with greased plastic wrap and let the dough rise until doubled in size.

Generously grease the inside of an 8½ x 4½-inch/900g loaf pan with oil.

As soon as the dough has risen, tip it out onto a flour-dusted work surface and roll it out to a rectangle 10 x 14 inches/25 x 35cm.

Brush the top with the sriracha, distribute the 8 squares of cheese evenly over the top, dot with a few slices of the pepperoni, and pop a basil leaf on top of each.

Now cut the rectangle into 8 equal squares. Take each square and fold it in half like a book. Stack them side by side in the pan with the filling bit exposed at the top. Then let rise, covered in greased plastic wrap, until it has doubled in size again.

Preheat the oven to 400°F.

Once the dough has risen, take off the plastic wrap and bake for 25 minutes.

Take it out of the oven and brush all over with olive oil, then let cool in the pan for 20 minutes before pulling apart and tearing and sharing!

polenta bake

Serves 6
Prep 25 minutes, plus chilling
Cook 50 minutes

For the polenta

olive oil, for greasing and brushing

1 quart/1 liter of water

1⅓ cups/225g coarsely ground polenta

½ teaspoon salt

½ teaspoon turmeric

2 teaspoons ground black pepper

¼ cup/50g unsalted butter

1¾ oz/50g mature Cheddar cheese, grated, + an extra 3½ oz/100g for the top

For the sauce

1 x 14-oz/397g can of evaporated milk

¾ cup + 2 tablespoons/200ml whole milk

7 oz/200g mature Cheddar, finely grated

1 tablespoon cornstarch

a pinch of salt

10½ oz/300g baby spinach leaves

4½ oz/120g salmon trimmings

The first time I tried polenta this way, it was the packaged kind. I probably didn't read the instructions properly, because it didn't turn out very well, or I did follow the instructions and it was just a lost cause. It doesn't have to be, as this is the kind of thing you can make yourself and set in advance, ready to be baked when you get home for tea. Mixed with cheese, it's a delicious alternative to potatoes or rice.

Let's make the polenta first. Grease and line an 8½ x 4½-inch/900g loaf pan with some plastic wrap.

Pour the water into a pan and bring to a boil. Put the polenta in a bowl with the salt, turmeric, and pepper and mix until evenly combined. Now, in a steady stream add the polenta mixture to the boiling water, turn the heat down, and mix. Keep stirring until it is really stiff and begins to come away from the pan. Now add the butter and the cheese and mix until combined.

Tip the mixture out into the prepared loaf pan and flatten the top. Let cool slightly and then chill in the fridge for about 4 hours, until firm.

Now start to make the cheese sauce by putting the evaporated milk into a small nonstick pot along with the milk. Stir and bring to a boil, then turn the heat down completely. In another bowl, mix the cheese with the cornstarch until the cheese is coated. Tip it into the milk mixture, along with the salt, and mix until you have a thick, cheesy sauce. Take off the heat.

Preheat the oven to 400°F. Oil the bottom and sides of a roasting dish (approximately 12 inches/30cm in diameter).

Take the polenta mixture and cut into ½-inch/1cm slices and arrange them in the roasting dish. It doesn't have to be an even layer; they can overlap a bit, it's fine. Lightly grease the top by brushing with olive oil and pop into the oven for 20 minutes to lightly crisp up the polenta.

Remove from the oven and pile the spinach right on top. Sprinkle with the salmon trimmings and pour the sauce over the top, then sprinkle over the extra grated cheese.

Place in the oven and bake for 30 minutes, until you have a delicious crisp, cheesy top. Let cool 10 minutes before eating.

cauliflower
cheese lasagne

Serves 6   Prep 30 minutes   Cook 1 hour

butter, for greasing

2¼ cups/500g mascarpone

2 tablespoons granulated garlic

1 medium onion, finely diced

1 teaspoon salt

1 teaspoon ground black pepper

7 tablespoons/100ml whole milk

12¼ oz/350g red leicester cheese, grated

a large handful of chives, chopped

2 small cauliflower heads, excluding stalks, thinly sliced (approx. 1¾ pounds/800g)

1 broccoli head, excluding stalk, thinly sliced (approx. 10½ oz/300g unprepped weight)

6 fresh lasagne sheets (½ a package)

This does what it says in the title. It's cauliflower cheese crossed with lasagne, that's it. So if you like both of those things, which I definitely do, then this one is for you, all for you.

Have a deep lasagne dish ready (10 x 8 x 3 inches/ 25 x 20 x 8cm). Grease the inside with some butter. Preheat the oven to 350°F.

Start by making the filling. Put the mascarpone in a large bowl along with the granulated garlic, onion, salt, pepper, and milk and mix well. Now add 7 oz/ 200g of the cheese and the chives and stir to combine well.

Combine the sliced cauliflower and broccoli in a microwaveable bowl with 1 tablespoon of water.

Cover with plastic wrap and cook for 7 to 8 minutes, until just soft. You may have to do this in two batches as there is rather a lot of veg. Add the cooked vegetables to the mascarpone mix, making sure not to add any excess liquid from the dish. Stir well.

Take a third of the mixture and spread evenly in the bottom of the lasagne dish. Add 3 lasagne sheets on top in a single layer to cover all the cauliflower mix, cutting them if necessary to make them fit.

Add the next third, cover with 3 lasagne sheets again, and then add the rest of the cauliflower mix.

Sprinkle with the remaining grated cheese and bake in the oven for 45 minutes, until the top is toasted and the center is piping hot. Just before serving, switch to broiler mode, to get some color on that lasagne top.

tarragon mushrooms and eggs on toast

Serves 6   Prep 15 minutes
Cook 25 minutes

For the mushrooms

6 tablespoons/90ml vegetable oil

3 cloves of garlic, crushed

1 medium onion, grated to a paste

6 portobello mushrooms, caps intact, stalks removed and chopped

½ teaspoon salt

1 teaspoon ground black pepper

1¼ cups/300ml heavy cream

a small handful of fresh tarragon, leaves chopped, or 1 tablespoon dried

6 large eggs

⅔ cup/70g breadcrumbs, fresh or dried

To serve

6 slices of toast

chopped chives

This is such a simple but hearty meal: quick, easy, and veggie too! Perfect for a delicious lunch, a lazy supper, or any kind of brunch, the mushrooms are cooked gently in the oven, covered in creamy tarragon sauce, and then topped with an egg and some breadcrumbs, before being baked again, ready to eat on crunchy toast.

Preheat the oven to 400°F.

Start with a roasting dish that is large enough to house 6 portobello mushrooms.

Put the oil, garlic, and onion in the dish and mix well with your hands. Drop in the chopped mushroom stalks and mix them in too.

Finally, add the mushroom caps and, using your hands again, give them a gentle mix to coat them in all that lovely flavor.

Sprinkle with salt and pepper and mix again. Position the mushrooms so the undersides of the caps are facing upward, then pop them into the oven to bake for 15 minutes.

Take the mushrooms out of the dish, add the cream and tarragon to the dish and stir. Return the mushroom caps and crack an egg into each one. You will find the egg will spill over, but that is totally all right. Sprinkle all over with breadcrumbs. Don't worry about the breadcrumbs getting everywhere; it helps to thicken the sauce. Season again.

Bake for 10 minutes more. If you don't like a runny yolk, bake for another 5 to 6 minutes.

Place a mushroom and egg on top of each piece of crunchy toast and be sure to dish up some of that delicious creamy sauce, too.

Sprinkle with chopped fresh chives before serving.

salt-and-pepper baked chicken and fries

Serves 4	Prep 40 minutes
Cook 2 hours	

For the chicken

1 small chicken, halved, skin on (3 pounds/1.4kg)

7 tablespoons/100ml whole milk

juice of ½ a lemon

1½ teaspoons salt

1 teaspoon ground turmeric

¾ cup/100g all-purpose flour

2 teaspoons ground black pepper

For the fries

2 pounds 2 oz/1kg small waxy potatoes, quartered lengthwise

3 tablespoons oil, + extra for greasing roasting dish

4 large cloves of garlic or 8 small, peeled and thinly sliced

1 tablespoon chile flakes, or less if you prefer

1 tablespoon ground black pepper

1 small red onion, thinly sliced

1 tablespoon sea salt flakes

This is "salt and pepper" chicken, like what you might find on the menu of a Chinese restaurant. Why not add fries alongside—especially when these ones are baked in the oven, making them easier and a little better for you than any from a deep fryer. Crisp chicken and spicy potatoes—sometimes that is all we need!

Put the chicken halves in a large pot of water, bring to a boil, and boil for 10 minutes. Take off the heat, drain, and let cool.

Now start making the buttermilk. Pour the milk into a bowl large enough to fit the chicken halves. Squeeze in the lemon juice and add 1 teaspoon of the salt and the turmeric. Mix and set aside for 10 minutes.

Once the chicken is cool, put it in the bowl with the buttermilk and smother it all over—get your hands right in there.

For the fries, boil the potatoes for 15 minutes. Remove from the heat and drain.

Put the oil into a nonstick pan and, as soon as it is hot, add the garlic and cook for a minute or two, until the slices just catch a little color.

Take off the heat and add the chile flakes, black pepper, onion, and sea salt, then stir to coat with the hot oil. Add the boiled potatoes and set aside.

Preheat the oven to 400°F.

Take a large roasting dish and drizzle in a little oil. If you don't have a large one, you might need to bake in two dishes—so half a chicken and some fries in each dish.

Combine the flour, the remaining ½ teaspoon salt, and the pepper on a plate and mix. Take the chicken out of the buttermilk mix and place facedown into the flour, making sure the flour coats any part that is covered with chicken skin. Put the pieces in the roasting dish skin-side up.

Scatter the potato mix all around the chicken, then cover the dish with foil and bake for 1 hour before removing the foil and cooking for another 30 minutes.

Take the roasting dish out of the oven and let the chicken cool slightly before serving.

baked ratatouille

For the meat layer

oil, for greasing

1 cup/250g uncooked tomato purée

1 pound 2 oz/500g ground lamb

1 beef stock cube, crushed to a powder

3 cloves of garlic, crushed

2 tablespoons dried parsley

1⅓ cups/150g dried breadcrumbs

For the ratatouille layer

3 large green zucchini, about 14 oz/400g, thinly sliced into ⅛-inch/3mm rounds

3 medium red onions, thinly sliced into ⅛-inch/3mm slices

6 large tomatoes, about 1 pound 2 oz/500g, thinly sliced into rounds

3 small eggplants, about 1 pound 5 oz/ 600g, thinly sliced into ⅛-inch/3mm rounds

3 x 4½-oz/125g mozzarella balls, thinly sliced into rounds, well drained and patted dry

For the oil

3 tablespoons olive oil

1 clove of garlic, crushed

1 teaspoon dried oregano

a sprinkling of ground black pepper

a sprinkling of salt

To serve

1¾ oz/50g Parmesan, finely grated

crusty bread (optional)

Serves 4
Prep 45 minutes
Cook 1½ hours

I like ratatouille because of the way it is cooked: slowly and usually all in one pot. This is a ratatouille made pretty—layered with ground lamb on the bottom and the beautiful vegetables on top, then smothered with oil and perfectly baked. All in one and delicious. Dinner's in the oven.

Preheat the oven to 350°F.

Grease the bottom and sides of a roasting dish (9 x 13 x 2 inches/23 x 30 x 5cm).

Put the tomato purée into the roasting dish with the ground lamb. Add the crushed stock cube, garlic, and dried parsley and mix thoroughly, then bake in the oven for 30 minutes, until the meat is cooked through.

Remove from the oven (keep it switched on) and sprinkle the breadcrumbs over the meat.

Layer your slices of vegetables, alternating between the zucchini, onions, tomatoes, eggplants, and mozzarella, until you have finished the lot and covered the meat and breadcrumbs completely.

In a small pan, gently heat the oil. Add the crushed garlic and heat until the garlic begins to sizzle. Take off the heat, add the oregano, and stir well.

Brush the top of the layered veg with the warm oil and when you have used it all up, sprinkle generously with the salt and pepper.

If you are making this in advance you can pop it in the fridge overnight until you are ready to bake. When ready, bake in the oven for 50 to 60 minutes, then sprinkle a light layer of grated Parmesan over the top and you are ready to go. Serve with a crusty loaf of bread, if desired.

teriyaki chicken noodles

For the teriyaki sauce

1¼ cups/300ml hot water

3 tablespoons brown sugar

½ cup + 2 tablespoons/ 150ml dark soy sauce

1 oz/30g ginger, not peeled, finely grated

6 cloves of garlic, crushed

1–2 teaspoons chile flakes (optional, or adjust to your taste)

5 boneless chicken thighs

8 oz/225g instant vermicelli noodles (5 nests)

To finish

a small handful of cilantro, chopped

3 green onions, thinly sliced

1 large red chile, sliced

sesame seeds, black and white

Serves 5 **Prep** 25 minutes, plus marinating
Cook 35 minutes

Any meal that produces as few dishes as possible to wash at the end I consider a success. Minimal washing-up, maximum smiles, and even more "mmms": these are my measures of a great recipe. This spicy, zingy, teriyaki noodle dish is exactly that—made with chicken thighs and all baked together in one roasting dish, it always results in lots of "yums," not to mention the question, "Did you just bake noodles?"Yes, I did. And when I say zingy, I do mean hot, so adjust the heat by taking out or decreasing the chile to your preference.

Begin by making the marinade. Mix the hot water and the sugar in a medium roasting dish, stirring to allow the sugar to melt and the water to cool. This should only take a few minutes.

Add the soy, ginger, garlic, and chile and mix well.

Next, add the chicken and let marinate for 30 minutes. You don't have to marinate at all if you are in a rush, but if you are cooking for the next day, then marinate in the sauce overnight and this will really soak into the chicken. Even a few hours will make a difference, if you have the time.

Preheat the oven to 400°F.

Bake the chicken for 25 minutes, until cooked through.

Take the chicken pieces out of the roasting dish, leaving the marinade behind. Add the 5 nests of noodles, flipping them over to coat them in the liquid. If your marinade has become quite dry, you can add up to another 1¼ cups/300ml of hot water.

Put a piece of chicken back on top of each noodle nest and then put back into the oven for 10 minutes to allow the noodles to absorb all that moisture.

Take out and garnish with the cilantro, green onions, red chile, and sesame seeds, and your chicken noodles are ready to eat.

peach-baked salmon

For the green beans

oil, for greasing

3 x 6-oz/170g packages of French green beans

½ cup/50g sliced almonds

For the salmon

1 pound 14 oz/850g side of salmon, skin removed

1 x 15-oz/420g can of peaches, drained (9 oz/250g)

¼ teaspoon cloves

1 teaspoon granulated garlic

½ teaspoon salt

½ teaspoon ground black pepper

⅔ cup/65g toasted golden breadcrumbs

For the dressing

3 tablespoons olive oil

2 tablespoons balsamic vinegar

2 fresh peaches, diced

Serves 6–8　**Prep** 25 minutes
Cook 25 minutes

I often cook a whole side of salmon when I have people coming over; it feels lovely to be able to place something quick, easy, and delicious in the center of the table. I am always holding out for leftovers for lunch the next day, but too often that is not the case. This fish is simple—lightly spiced with a clove and peach sauce, baked on a bed of delicious roasted French beans and almonds, and dressed with balsamic and fresh peaches.

Preheat the oven to 400°F and have ready a roasting dish that can comfortably fit the salmon.

Drizzle some oil in the dish. Halve the green beans and drop them straight in.

Add the almonds, then, using your hands, combine them really well and flatten to an even layer.

Place the salmon right on top.

Put the drained peaches in a food processor, along with the cloves, garlic, salt, and pepper. Whiz to a smooth paste.

Add the breadcrumbs and whiz very briefly again to combine.

Spoon the mixture in an even layer all over the top of the salmon, before putting it in the oven to bake for 25 minutes.

Make the dressing by mixing the oil and balsamic in a bowl that's suitable to use an immersion blender in. Add 2 tablespoons of the diced peaches and whiz to a smooth dressing. Add the remaining cubes of peach to the dressing and mix really well.

As soon as the salmon is done, place it gently on a serving platter.

Arrange the green beans around the side of the fish. Drizzle the dressing all over the beans and salmon and you are ready to eat.

baked rice and eggs

For the rice

1½ cups/300g basmati rice

1 cup + 2 tablespoons/ 140g unsalted butter, melted

1 teaspoon salt

1 teaspoon ground turmeric

2 teaspoons ground white pepper

1 lemon, finely grated zest and juice

14 oz/400g frozen green beans

2½ cups/600ml hot water

For the eggs

6 large eggs

3 green onions, chopped

a small handful of cilantro, chopped

a pinch of salt

paprika for sprinkling

Serves 6   **Prep** 20 minutes
Cook 1 hour 45 minutes

This recipe goes against everything I was taught about rice: that it is always cooked on a stovetop and never in an oven, even a fancy rice dish like a biryani, which is placed in a massive pan (I'm talking large enough to fit a grown human) and precariously set against all four burners, heat on the edges but not in the center. It's always a juggling act, but no one ever deployed the oven. So why not? Let's do it. For anyone nervous about cooking rice, with this recipe you needn't be, as it's simple, easy, and all done in the oven, for a great taste with no worries.

Preheat the oven to 350°F.

Start with a serving dish 8¼ x 8¼ inches/21 x 21cm. Glass is ideal so you can see the rice cook, but use whatever you have at home. Put the rice in the dish.

Mix the melted butter with the salt, turmeric, and pepper and stir together until totally combined.

Add the zest of the lemon and mix it in. Add this mixture to the rice and combine well.

Spread your frozen green beans evenly on top of the uncooked rice. Now pour the hot water carefully on top, making sure not to disturb the peace. Cover with foil and bake in the oven for 30 minutes.

Take off the foil and bake for another 30 minutes uncovered.

Meanwhile, break the eggs into a bowl, add the green onions, cilantro, and salt and mix really well.

When the rice comes out of the oven, squeeze the lemon juice all over it and drop in the egg mixture. Sprinkle generously with paprika and bake again, uncovered, for 15 to 20 minutes, until the eggs are cooked.

Take out and let cool for 5 minutes before digging in.

spiced squash strudel

For the filling

3 tablespoons
vegetable oil

2 tablespoons coriander
seeds, crushed

3 cloves of garlic, crushed

1 pound 2 oz/500g
butternut squash, diced

1 lemon, finely grated zest
and juice

½ teaspoon salt

½ teaspoon ground
cinnamon

1 teaspoon paprika

⅓ cup/50g cashews,
roughly chopped

⅓ cup/50g currants

a large handful of
cilantro, leaves chopped

For the strudel

1 pound 2 oz/500g puff
pastry block

1 egg, beaten

sea salt

Serves 6   **Prep** 30 minutes, plus cooling
Cook 1 hour 30 minutes

I do love a classic apple strudel, but a savory variety can be just as delicious, especially as the leftovers can be eaten cold afterward. This one is made simply with store-bought puff pastry and filled with a spiced butternut squash mixture.

Start by making the filling, because it needs to cool before the strudel can be assembled.

Warm the oil in a large nonstick sauté pan and, as soon as it is hot, add the coriander seeds. When they begin to sizzle, add the garlic and cook for about 2 minutes, until golden brown.

Add the squash and stir to coat in the garlicky oil.

Add the lemon zest and juice, plus the salt, cinnamon, and paprika and mix well. Cover with the lid, decrease the heat to low and cook until there is no liquid left and the squash is totally soft; this should take about 40 minutes.

Take off the heat and transfer to a bowl to cool. Mash using the back of a fork.

Add the cashews, currants, and cilantro and mix well. Set aside until totally cooled.

Take your puff pastry block and roll into a rectangle 10 x 8 inches/25 x 20cm. Pop onto a baking sheet lined with some parchment paper and let chill in the fridge for 15 minutes.

Preheat the oven to 400°F and put a baking sheet into the oven to heat up. Take the pastry out and place with the shortest side closest to you. Brush the edges with egg.

Add the filling down the center, in the middle third of the pastry. Fold over one third and then the other third. You should have a seam running down the center. Seal the ends. Now gently flip the strudel over so the seam is on the bottom.

Brush all over with the egg, make a small slit in the center to allow steam to escape, sprinkle with salt, and bake for 40 to 45 minutes on top of the hot sheet. If after 35 minutes the pastry is getting too dark, turn down to 350°F and cover loosely with foil.

Let cool for 10 minutes before digging in.

thanks

Nothing seems sweeter than writing a whole entire book about baking and truthfully there is a joy that I have found in writing this book that has made me realize what I love about baking and what it does for me apart from produce something sweet to eat.

I want to thank the person who decided that throwing some butter, eggs, flour, and sugar together would be a good idea, because, boy, were you right, whoever you are, however far back in history you are from. Thank you! You will not read this or know of this, but we all thank you for the gift that is cake!

Thank you to our recipe tester, Katy, for the high-lighting, the note-making, and the deleting of my repetitive words, but most of all thank you for the little notes on top that would read "that was delicious"—as that is what really makes me happy!

Thank you, Chris Terry, for your beautiful photography. You are hired for your art *and* your dry sense of humor, as a package, so remember to put that on top of your packing list.

Thank you, Georgia Glynn Smith of N5 Studios.

To Rob Allison and Rosie MacKean, thank you for all the work you guys put in to getting the food prim, proper, and photo-ready every single time. Thanks for not hating me when I say, "Shall we do that one again?"

To Roya, for your beautiful eye and attention to detail, thank you.

Anne, just always there, tapping, meddling, eating, and repeating!

Thank you, Dan and Ione, for being as excited about this book as I was and for believing in it always. Dan, while you just keep powering through the food, Ione and I will be all over the spreadsheets!

Thank you to the entire team, especially Bea for our back and forth—it never annoys me—I promise, and Sarah for coming up with the most extraordinary designs, I am wowed every time! Thank you to Claire Bush, Laura Nicol, Beth O'Rafferty, Agatha Russell, Annie Lee, Gail Jones, Dan Prescott-Bennett, Heather B, and everyone else for being a part of this mammoth process—we did it!

Thank you all. We have worked tirelessly to breathe joy into the book and bring it well and truly to life. For the exchanged emails in the wee hours of the night. For looking at the same thing over and over and over again till all you see is a blur. For those who have eaten, dropped, and amended recipes.

Thank you, Abdal, Musa, Dawud, and Maryam: for always eating cake, for as long as you will eat cake, I will bake it!

index

c

Published in the United States by Clarkson Potter/Publishers, an imprint
of Random House, a division of Penguin Random House LLC, New York.
clarksonpotter.com

CLARKSON POTTER is a trademark and POTTER with colophon is a
registered trademark of Penguin Random House LLC.

Originally published in hardcover in Great Britain by
Michael Joseph, a division of Penguin Random House Ltd.,
London, in 2020. By arrangement with the BBC.

Library of Congress Cataloging-in-Publication Data
LC record available at lccn.loc.gov/2021004506.
LC ebook record available at lccn.loc.gov/2021004507.

ISBN 978-0-593-23373-3
Ebook ISBN 978-0-593-23374-0

Printed in China

10 9 8 7 6 5 4 3 2 1

First American Edition